The Raim

David V. Tansley was a Doctor of Chiropr leading authority on radionics and distant healing. He made an extensive study of the subtle anatomy of man and its relationship to various healing techniques, and conducted workshops on this subject worldwide. He also lectured on parapsychology at the University of Western Australia, and at Murdoch University, Perth, Western Australia. His books include *Radionics and the Subtle Anatomy of Man* (1972), *Omens of Awareness* (1977) and *Subtle Body – Essence and Shadow* (1976). He died in 1988.

DAVID V. TANSLEY

THE RAIMENT
OF LIGHT

A STUDY OF THE
HUMAN AURA

FOREWORD BY MICHAEL BENTINE

ARKANA

ARKANA

Published by the Penguin Group
27 Wrights Lane, London W8 5TZ, England
Viking Penguin Inc., 40 West 23rd Street, New York, New York 10010, USA
Penguin Books Australia Ltd, Ringwood, Victoria, Australia
Penguin Books Canada Ltd, 2801 John Street, Markham, Ontario, Canada L3R 1B4
Penguin Books (NZ) Ltd, 182–190 Wairau Road, Auckland 10, New Zealand

Penguin Books Ltd, Registered Offices: Harmondsworth, Middlesex, England

First published by Routledge & Kegan Paul Ltd 1983
Published by Arkana 1985
3 5 7 9 10 8 6 4

Printed and bound in Great Britain by
Cox & Wyman Ltd, Reading

Contents

Acknowledgments   viii

Foreword by Michael Bentine   ix

1   The raiment of light   1
2   The vital force revisited   21
3   Subtle bodies, chakras and the aura   42
4   Science and medicine look at the aura   65
5   Colours of the auric field   91
6   Sensing, seeing and reading the human aura   110
7   Dowsing and the human aura   132
8   Auric pollution — physical and psychic   145
9   Cleansing and healing the aura   159
10 The influence of gems   174
11 A radiance of light and love and power   184

Bibliography   192

Index   195

Illustrations

Figure 1.1   Electro photograph showing coronal
              discharge around the human hand   12
Figure 1.2   Electro photograph of abdomen and lower
              thorax   13
Figure 1.3   Coronal discharge around a coin and a key 14
Figure 3.1   The large ovoid field of energy around
              the head and shoulders is a manifesta-
              tion of psychic energy   49
Figure 3.2   The psycho-magnetic curving lines of
              force which surround the human head   59
Figure 4.1   The outline of a healthy male aura
              according to Kilner   66
Figure 4.2   Transverse sections of male and female
              auras according to Kilner (a) and (b)
              normal auras; (c) and (d) spatulate
              auras; (e) and (f) auras with dorsal
              bow-shaped bulge   68
Figure 5.1   A model of the ray energies in an
              individual   100
Figure 6.1   Itch points and their basic significance
              (a) Some of the itch points on the head
              and face; (b) Front view of the body
              showing itch points   122-3

Figure 7.1   Aura of a healthy male subject   135
Figure 8.1   Illustration by Kilner of the effect of
              negatively electrifying aura, causing
              the outer shell to expand   146
Figure 8.2   Pathological appearance of aura as seen
              through the Kilner Screen. Granular
              textures and holes appear in the auric
              field   148
Figure 8.3   Loss of continuity of inner aura
              following an appendectomy   151
Figure 9.1   Ritual of Light   166

Acknowledgments

I would like to thank my wife Elizabeth for her constant encouragement during the writing of this book, in the process of which we travelled half way round the world and back. My thanks and deepest gratitude to Jean Meade who kindly provided us with a haven, a twenty-mile view across the Sussex countryside, and a close proximity to the 'aura' of H.G. Wells. There is no doubt the peace and inspiration drawn from our surroundings helped to keep me at the typewriter.

I am also grateful to Dr Julian Kenyon, MD, and the Centre for the Study of Alternative Therapies for permission to reproduce figures 1.1, 1.2 and 1.3.

Foreword

David Tansley is an enthusiastic seeker with an open mind. He reads avidly with a voracious appetite for unusual and original concepts of life and nature. This book is a broad review of many such ideas and some readers may not agree with a number of its statements. However such a book is a sign that our times are changing rapidly. Today's structure of scientific thought requires revision to accommodate a number of ideas touched upon by the author. I believe we need such mental stimuli to break the bonds of our present destructive, materialistic thinking, which surely is leading us towards global self-immolation.

Michael Bentine

For Daron
and
to the memory of
Adrian Boshier

who stood between two worlds,
and in the true tradition of
the shaman showed me the heart
of Africa

1

The raiment of light

The experience itself was one of an amazing bright light
in the form of an inward illumination, not of a kind detectable by the eye, but one was seeing things and people in
a way not previously experienced. They were seen lit up
as though in a glow.

A Sense of Presence — Timothy Beardsworth

If you have felt an indefinable sense of discomfort whilst
in the presence of an individual, something you couldn't
quite put your finger on that left you ill at ease, or basked
in the soft peaceful atmosphere of a forest clearing in late
summer, with the warm air and the lazy distant drone of
insects perceptibly opening a door to another dimension
of consciousness, then you have sensed the aura. To stand
in the aisle of an ancient church or cathedral and allow the
accumulated power of a thousand years of prayer to uplift
you with a force that can bring exultation and a sense of
peace, is to touch upon the aura. We have all experienced
these alterations of awareness. They are in fact so common
that we rarely give them a second thought, and in this
manner we fail to register a whole spectrum of information
that is constantly being made available to us through the

higher aspects of our physical senses. We narrow our world through our lack of attention. In the words of Yaqui sorcerer Don Juan, we indulge, we are loose in our observations, scattered and vulnerable. In such a state our aura picks up all manner of negative energies from the people around us, from the media and from places and states of consciousness we have wandered into through lack of attention. To be aware of the aura is to adopt the stance of the warrior, knowing every thought and action to be significant, leaving little to chance and seeing the world in a different way.

All forms, be they human, animal, plant, or even the apparently inert mineral, radiate a surrounding field of energy into the environment. This field or aura expresses the quality and nature of the form which it interpenetrates and surrounds. In other words it carries information which can be registered by sensitives to provide knowledge with respect to persons, places and objects. To a greater or lesser degree we all have this sensitivity, this innate capacity to register invisible energy fields. In some it is more highly developed; these people we call psychics or clairvoyants. For most people, however, the ability tends to remain, as it were, below a certain level of awareness, rarely intruding into the conscious mind of the individual, or when it does, being suppressed in an instant reflex action. This is true of many people today who for one reason or another have shut down or inhibited their psychic sensitivity.

We live in a society that does little to encourage awareness of the invisible, and in fact sets out actively to discourage those who exhibit such capacities. Children, for example, are often ridiculed if they say they have seen something that is not apparent to their elders, and in time many learn either to keep quiet or actually to shut off this natural gift of sensitivity. Many years ago my young daughter was standing in the kitchen of our house when she suddenly said 'What's that man doing there?', pointing to an empty area of the room. Then, looking puzzled, she said 'He walked through the wall into the garden next door. He's gone!' She found it quite easy to accept the simple explanation that people can function out of their physical body at times, and that they would appear as this man had to her. After all she had seen him in a natural and spontaneous way; to have ridiculed her or told her not to be silly would have begun the process of stifling her sensitivity and teaching her not to trust her own senses.

In the preface of his book *Psychic Children*, Samuel Young writes of an eight-year-old girl who could see colours around people as a fluid, multi-hued field which she related to people's moods. In class one day she and some classmates were misbehaving behind the teacher's back when she noticed a build up of red flaring patches around the teacher's head. She took this to mean anger and immediately resumed her work. The teacher suddenly turned and caught the others in the act of playing about. Many children see auras in this manner as a matter of course and those who retain this capacity into adulthood almost always recall that they thought everybody saw such things, but found sooner or later that this was not the case.

There can be little doubt that prehistoric man had this type of uncomplicated sensitivity and depended heavily upon his ability to see or sense the aura. To him it meant survival, the one dominant theme that pervaded his life. It was essential for him to know what was going on, not only in his immediate envirionment but at a distance too, through what we may describe as a form of radiatory energy affinity which enabled him to determine the presence of game at a distance or identify the location of predators who might be waiting to strike him down. In his book *Divining the Primary Sense*, Herbert Weaver writes:

Reflexive response to sympathetic particle- or wave-interchange in the chemical radiating regions of the spectrum was the birthright of early man before he allowed that sense to degenerate.

Prehistoric man lived in a totally unpolluted environment in which all life-forms constantly interacted in terms of reciprocal energy exchanges. Thus any life-form, bird, animal, or reptile, flora and minerals, from the blades of grass underfoot to the very soil itself, formed with man a vast symphonic field of energies. This environmental aura was a vast mosaic of constantly changing energies, and it served in effect as an energy data bank through and into which each could send querying probes of energy in order to elicit information from the field through a form of reciprocal resonance. Roaming herds of grazing animals might modify their auras for one moment to resonate with the auric patterns of lush grass, and through the interplay be drawn to it, and in another moment to the waveform of predators that they might avoid them. Predators in their turn applied the same principles to identify and locate game. Man, through his ability to add the process of thought to energy field identification at a distance, soon moved into a position of domination and learned to probe and decipher these auric fields to his own advantage. Weaver writes of these signal patterns as radiational couriers, stating that they inspire migratory movements of wildlife and prod hibernators into wakefulness.

Homing and the distant location of prey depend also on chemical direction. However if there were no counter to faunal searching vectors projected by every hunting creature, most species would have become extinct long ago, having been systematically exterminated by a succession of unrestricted predators drawn from great distances to the young shoots of a plantation or to the eggs of bird colonies.

Weaver has some interesting things to say regarding the

way in which energy fields in nature can be modified or suppressed.

Nature's conservation counter to the hunting vector lay in the evolution of certain two-dimensional signs and three-dimensional sign-structures, of which flora may have first produced the archetypes in the twig and leaf. The natural suppressors of food signals throw a protective mantle of paramagnetic force-fields over or around each plant or resting animal, suppressing the involuntary broadcast of untimely pollination advertisement or self-betraying protein radiation.

Arboreal man employed the protective effects of fortuitously found crossed twigs and leaf-pattern alignments to confine his chemical emissions which would otherwise have betrayed his presence; primitive man was constantly exposed to distant detection by ferocious animals, especially during unguarded times of rest.

Through careful observation and experimentation prehistoric man soon learned that certain archetypal protective patterns could be re-created with pigments and painted on the walls of caves, or on his own body, in such a manner that they rendered him 'invisible' to the distant monitoring of predators. In other words he found a method of damping down the radiation of his aura which gave him a distinct advantage over other predators. Today we may confuse this type of 'invisibility' with optical invisibility but it has nothing to do with this at all. Plants were also employed to shut down the auric field and in folk lore we read that amaranth, mistletoe and the seeds of fern and monkshood confer 'invisibility'.

Ancient man was a highly sensitive being with remarkable cognitive powers and intellectual capacity covering a wide range of symbolic comprehension as evidenced in his incredibly fine art and rich aesthetic tradition.

6/The raiment of light

In his book *The Silent Pulse*, George Leonard writes:

> For it's clear that members of surviving primitive
> hunting and gathering bands possess sensing abilities
> foreign to most of us, abilities to sense underground
> water in desert areas, to find direction and locate
> position on cloudy days, and, in some cases, to 'view'
> game animals that are out of range of the conventional
> senses.

Cave art clearly depicts prehistoric man's awareness of
the aura, many figures drawn on cave walls or rock faces
are surrounded by halo-like fields or radiating lines stick-
ing out at right angles to the body. Some drawings just
show the halo around the head while in others the whole
body is surrounded by bristling lines of force. Such art
can be found throughout the world, so universal was this
awareness of the aura and sensitivity to these fields. Some
of the most beautiful cave and rock art in the world is
to be found in Australia, drawn by Aborigines, and it is
interesting to note here that the true Aborigine when
he wanted to gather information from the environmental
aura, spoke of 'leaning on the wind'. This is such a beautiful phrase, redolent with meaning and so expressive of the
subtlety of the whole gentle process of tuning into the
life-field of nature, and the blending of the human aura
with it in one uncomplicated simplicity. The resultant
state of resonance gave the hunter-gatherer a unique sense
of relationship with all he surveyed both physically and
psychically. We shall later return to the Aborigine for he
has interesting things to tell us regarding the reading of
auras.

The phrase 'leaning on the wind' has a curious yet
perhaps not unexpected sympathy with the Greek word
avria, meaning breeze, from which the word aura derives.
Somehow it conjures up visions of the human form surrounded by an ever moving, swirling field of energy filled
with a kaleidoscope of shifting and changing colours, and

this indeed is how many psychics view the human aura. One of the most famous of these, Edgar Cayce, wrote in his booklet *Auras*:

> Ever since I can remember I have seen colors in connection with people. I do not remember a time when the human beings I encountered did not register on my retina with blues and greens and reds gently pouring from their heads and shoulders. It was a long time before I realized that other people did not see these colors; it was a long time before I heard the word aura, and learned to apply it to this phenomenon which to me was commonplace. I do not even think of people except in connection with their auras; I see them change in my friends and loved ones as time goes by — sickness, dejection, love, fulfillment — these are all reflected in the aura, and for me the aura is the weathervane of the soul. It shows me the way the winds of destiny are blowing.

We shall see in the course of this book that the various colours appearing in the aura express information with respect to the individual's past, present and future life. Health is clearly depicted through the clarity and types of colour present, as is character and spiritual aspiration. Past accidents can be seen and future disease processes indentified by the skilled clairvoyant, as he or she views the human aura with inner sight.

Since time immemorial man has illustrated the aura to express the spiritual nature of man. For example, in Christian art the halo or nimbus around the head is a common feature filled with meaning for those with sufficient ability to decipher what is being portrayed. If you look carefully you will see that the nimbus around the head of Jesus differs from those placed around the heads of the disciples. A plain unadorned disc of colour behind the head indicates a dormant or latent principle. Little lines extending around the disc show an awakening spirituality. Straight lines radiating out from the halo symbolize the power of the sun or soul, and curved lines indicate the lunar forces of the lower-self. The halo of Jesus often shows a cross within it to illustrate his direct and completely unobstructed contact with the Logos.

The aura may also be represented by the type of head-gear or dress worn. The North American Indian bonnet of eagle feathers, cresting the head and flowing down the back, is a beautiful badge of rank and spiritual status, factors which at one time went hand in hand. Further-more, the wearing of eagle feathers may well have brought added power and brilliance to the aura of the chief as he sat in council bringing his influence to bear on tribal matters. In many such societies the eagle is looked upon as a symbol of the soul, regal, alert and powerful with the ability to soar on high. Consider the headgear worn by the Pharaohs of ancient Egypt, conical in shape, bearing the head of a snake or the high pointing psychic sensor shaped like the curled proboscis of a butterfly. In the history of the Christian church popes and bishops have worn hats of similar shape in order to enhance their auric fields. Kings and queens down through the ages have adorned their heads with crowns containing precious jewels, especially diamonds which are a symbol of high inner states of consciousness. These surely added to the clarity and beauty of the wearer's aura, particularly on state occasions when they wanted to 'shine out' and to be 'seen' by the populace. Today we have largely lost sight of these concepts but still wear ornaments of precious metals containing precious or semi-precious stones which must in various ways influence our auric fields. Care born of knowledge should dictate our choice in these matters lest we introduce the wrong stones or metals into our auras and disrupt the harmonious flow of energies therein. Man has always believed that precious and semi-precious stones were filled with mystic virtues which if placed in contact with the body would enhance the health, character and the fortunes of those who wore them. Chinese mandarins, for instance, wore stones to designate their rank: rubies and red tourmaline for those of the first rank, coral or garnet for the second, beryl or lapis for the third, rock-crystal for the fourth and other white stones for the fifth. The Japanese see the rock-crystal as the perfect jewel, a symbol of purity and the infinity of space. To the Aboriginal shaman it is a power object with many uses in sorcery. For thousands of years it has been used for scrying or seeing into the future, the crystal ball acting as a window to other levels of consciousness. Today the quartz crystal is high in popularity with many lay healers and some health care professionals who are involved in the more esoteric aspects of alternative healing methods, because it can apparently be used to focus and direct the power of thought to vitalize the aura and heal the body.

Physicians in the past have put great store on the use of precious and semi-precious stones to bring harmony to the invisible bodies of man, not least of these the sixteenth century alchemist and physician Paracelsus. He spoke and wrote about the vital force that filled man and radiated around him like a luminous sphere, the energy of which could be used in all manner of ways, particularly for healing. Visible forms, he said, were merely expressions of invisible principles and powers. Paracelsus called this invisible principle of life *Archeus* or *Liquor Vitae*, the subtle essence which formed the invisible man who indwelt the physical form. Elsewhere he speaks of the *Aura Seminalis*, each drop of which contained the image and likeness of the whole man. Such a concept ties in with modern holographic theories regarding human consciousness and the functions of mind and brain. A holograph is a three dimensional image that can be recorded on a plate by passing a laser beam of light through prisms and lenses. The remarkable thing about the image on the plate is that if you break the plate into pieces each piece will contain the whole image. It has been suggested that consciousness is rather like the holographic plate, in that each of us contains all of the information available, past, present and future. As we are a part of the whole, in theory we have access to all that has happened, is happening and will happen. Thus a psychic can 'see' events happening beyond time and space as we know it because those data exist in his own consciousness, which is a fragment of the whole.

The ability of Aborigines to track people is legendary, and it would appear that they quite instinctively apply the holographic principle. For experiment purposes a tracker has been told to retrace the path taken by a man many years previously, and with unerring accuracy he has been able to do this. In the North-West area of Canarvon, it is believed that the magician or shaman has a 'divided toe' which enables him to 'see' through his feet and to pick up the invisible tracks of people. The 'divided toe' or 'split toe' as it is also called might just have the same function as the Bealy Splitter which splits the coherent or single beam of light in holographic photography.

So far we have looked very briefly at what is called the vitalist view point. The vitalist theory states that some indefinable 'life-force' or non-physical entity animates the physical form we perceive with the physical senses and brings it to life, or literally gives life to it, and that this interaction between the life-force and form gives rise to emanations or a radiatory field known as the aura. The vitalist theory emerges from prehistory and may well be as old as man himself. It is to be found in one form or another in all cultures and societies throughout the world and pervades most religious belief systems in one guise or another.

In medicine we find Hippocrates and his peers speaking of mysterious fluid-like energies which flowed through the body, and references to the *augoeides* or aura of light around the human form are frequent. Galen likewise supported the concept of these fluid-like energies or humours, and attributed disease to the lack of flow and balance of this mysterious substance. By 1600 an English physician with a penchant for experimentation established the differences between electricity and magnetism, and in fact was the first to use the word electricity and set forth the idea of magnetic fields. Despite this, the vitalist theory still held sway, but the scene was set for its apparent demise as various experiments with electricity and biological specimens took place. Stephen Hales, an English clergyman of the 1700s, suggested that the nervous system worked by conducting 'electrical powers'. It was clear that the entity or spirit electricity was lining up to displace the entity of the 'vital spirit' or life-force. The scientific world of the day was divided and as much controversy as experimentation was to rage throughout Europe and Britain as such brilliant men as Luigi Galvani of Bologna, Allesandro Volta, professor of physics at Pavia in Italy, and his nephew Giovanni Aldini and others struggled to solve the mysteries of the connection between electricity, magnetism and biology. Despite all of their efforts, almost six decades later in the mid 1800s the vitalist doctrine still held pride of place. Finally towards the end of the century it was to give way, and it was not long before the work of such men as Julius Bernstein and von Helmholtz led the latter to proclaim that there were only physical and chemical forces acting in organisms, and that in effect man was nothing but a machine. The pendulum of opinion had swung to the opposite extreme, the vitalist theory of a life-force was considered superstitious nonsense. Science it seemed had the answer to the mystery of life, and as far as science was concerned that was that.

It is a curious fact that all intrinsic truths have a way of resurfacing and intruding themselves on the current scene, particularly if the period in question is lacking in breadth of vision regarding the real purpose of life. Such an intrusion manifested in the form of the electro-dynamic theory of life as put forward by Saxton Burr and Northrop

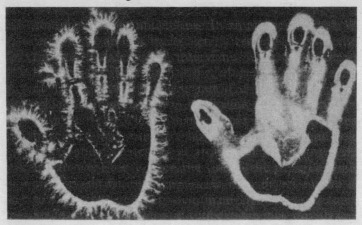

Figure 1.1 Electro photograph showing coronal discharge around the human hand

in 1935. As we shall see later it has amazing similarities to the concepts outlined in ancient texts relative to the etheric or vital body and the human aura. Needless to say, despite its validity in scientific terms many scientists have done their best to avoid it and turned away from the challenge it contains to their current beliefs, and have chosen to disregard the implications it bears relative to the unity of all life-forms, a most significant factor in the world of today.

Another intrusion took the form of electro-photography, which due to the work of Kirlians in Russia became very popular in the 1970s, and was subsequently hailed by those of a vitalist disposition as scientific proof of the life-force. As far as they were concerned the human aura had finally been captured on film and in colour, proof at last that the aura existed. By this time more and more scientists were beginning to feel and clearly see the need for esoteric philosophical concepts to be linked to current scientific ones, and a great deal of experimentation took place towards this end.

As the initial euphoria died down Kirlian photography

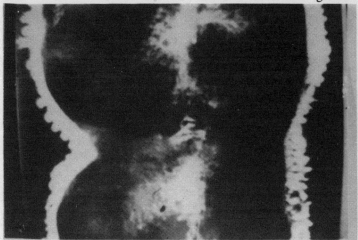

Figure 1.2 Electro photograph of abdomen and lower thorax

came under careful scrutiny, and many arguments were put forward to show that it was simply a physical phenomenon, and that the coronal discharge was not in fact the aura of the vitalists. I wonder if this really matters in the long term? What seems important to me is that, irrespective of the nature of the coronal discharge, it is an aura of some kind or other, and that in itself will prompt people to open their minds to consider further possibilities that may well have remained submerged by the sheer weight of scientific opinion. Kirlian photography has given us the term bioplasmic body, which is once again a concept that appears to bear a resemblance to the vital body described in the Vedas of ancient India, and the sidereal body found in the writings of Paracelsus.

According to all of those people who can view the human aura, it contains a wide spectrum of energies. At the lower end of the scale and easily measurable with modern instrumentation is the electro-magnetic aspect. Beyond that it rises through the infra-red range and continues up to the ultra-violet and into invisibility. Certain aspects of the aura can be seen with the naked eye, although

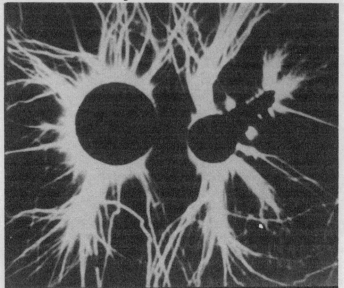

Figure 1.3 Coronal discharge around a coin and a key

this may take some practice. More subtle and rarefied qualities appear when the retinal rods of the eye have been sensitized by looking through a chemical substance known as dicyanin. Dr Walter Kilner made extensive use of this technique in his researches into the human aura at St Thomas's Hospital in London in the 1930s. Irrespective of how the aura is viewed, be it through dicyanin screens or by direct clairvoyant vision, it is seen to bear the qualities of light and hold information about the individual that is not available to the regular senses.

Whereas the scientist who is bound by orthodox concepts would say that the electro-magnetic spectrum of energies of the body has nothing to do with the aura as viewed by clairvoyants, I do not think that the latter would dismiss the idea. It is a fact that a larger viewpoint can always encompass the smaller without any real sense of discomfort, and as we shall see there is room in this field for a variety of beliefs and theories regarding the aura. Modern science might feel that it has layed the vitalist theory to rest, but the truth is that more and more evidence is coming to the fore which suggests we shall see a renaissance in this area. Saxton Burr and Northrop's work and the more recent advent of Kirlian photography has made people take another look at vitalism, and the great upsurge of interest in acupuncture that has touched even orthodox medicine, based as it is upon the manipulation of the life-force or *chi* as it is called in China, has further breached the walls of scientific dogma, bringing to our attention once again the ancient theories regarding the energy fields of man. More recently the concepts brought forward in physics, particularly quantum mechanics, are tentatively supplying supportive data that appear to have a direct correlation to the teachings of the mystics regarding the nature of life and the universe, teachings which orthodox science had dismissed out of hand a long time ago.

Although you may not be able to see auras, just being aware of them, especially your own, is a most important aspect of becoming centred. When you are centred you are in a state of harmony within; this creates a vital aura filled with the right blend of energies, an aura which extends outwards with a clarity that excludes negative impressions. We have all met people who seem literally to sparkle with energy and radiate vitality. Others, even if we are not clairvoyant, look as though they are surrounded by dull clouds. Lethargy, listlessness and a sense of heaviness pervade their auras, and we hasten to leave their company before we too are enveloped and affected by their drabness.

As members of a modern technological society we are subjected to many varied influences, a lot of them harmful to our health. Some affect our physical bodies directly and then the aura; others permeate the aura directly and have a profound influence on our psychological and physical health. Compare for example the auras of such cities as London, New York, Los Angeles and Tokyo with the aura of the high desert in California, the African veldt, or a remote glen in Scotland and you will begin to see what I mean. You only have to cast your mind back twenty years and compare the auras of London or San Francisco of those days to their present state. It's quite frightening. To be in a city means that your aura is subjected to a high level of physical and psychic pollution and the sheer pressure of stress in the atmosphere generated by human life takes its toll. It is important to know how to deal with this in a quiet and constructive manner, and this is something I will go into further on in the book.

The natural electro-magnetic field of the earth is not something we pay much attention to, and I am sure very few of us consider it in terms of pollution. The atmosphere of course is another thing, and pollution at that level through industrial waste, exhaust fumes, smog and the like is to the forefront of our awareness. But what of the electro-magnetic atmosphere? In their book *Electromagnetism and Life*, Drs Becker and Marino write:

> The environment is now thoroughly polluted by man-made sources of electromagnetic radiation with frequencies and magnitudes never before present. Man's activities have probably changed the earth's electromagnetic background to a greater degree than they have changed any other natural physical attribute of the earth — whether the land, water or atmosphere. The evidence now indicates that the present abnormal electromagnetic environment can constitute a health risk.

As you sit reading these words you are surrounded and interpenetrated by a whole range of radio waves, the transmissions from television stations, and if you are near an airport or military installation, you can add frequencies from radar to the list. So pervasive are all of these waves that at one time people used to pick up and hear radio broadcasts through the fillings in their teeth.

These waves of energy entering your aura are just a part of the whole situation. Consider for a moment the fact that your aura is an integral part of the aura of the planet earth, and you will begin to realize that conflict and desecration of natural resources and human life anywhere on this planet are not distant from you. Violence, physical or psychological, to any life-form, happening to someone or to someplace, will send reverberations rippling against your aura, and if you are especially sensitive and psychically open those patterns of violence will flood into your aura. Nothing happens outside of you if the holographic model of consciousness holds true, and so you may feel an unexplainable sense of fear or moment of panic or depression. For the most part we deal with these impressions by instinctively detuning and desensitizing our auras; we have to in order to survive the present level of psychic pollution engendered by man's lack of reverence for life. Just as people who live next to a railway track can tune out the noise of trains going by, so each of us, especially in the great cities, desensitize our auras and reduce the quality of our consciousness and our lives in the process. The end result is daily becoming more self-evident, the dehumanizing of man on an unprecedented scale and world tension the likes of which man has never seen before.

Of course there is another side to this apparently gloomy situation. The sheer pressure on humanity has caused many to seek solutions for the dilemma. The pollution of the earth's aura or biosphere, call it what you will, is both physical and psychic. The ecologists and environmentalists are attracted to the physical aspects of planetary pollution, and make their bid through protest and legislation to stem the tide of destruction unleashed on our natural resources. They have gained ground with the Clean Air Act, and reforestation projects on a worldwide scale are helping to restore some balance to the flora and fauna.

In the area of health care there is an unprecedented move towards alternative methods of healing. While drugs have their place in the scheme of things, the wholesale pollution of people's bodies with medication must surely rank as the crime of all time. People are recognizing the destructive side-effects of medically prescribed drugs, and the more perceptive are seeking to find health through natural methods of balanced diets and proper exercise. Vitamins and minerals are an important part of good nutrition, and it does help if diet is backed up with such nutritional substances. The growing interest in vitamins is indicative of a deepening inner awareness of the vital or etheric body. Vitamins as the name suggests do carry therapeutic amounts of specific aspects of the life-force, they help to vitalize the etheric body and thus increase resistance to disease.

Another indication of our attempt to balance our auric forces is the unprecedented worldwide interest in human consciousness and awareness. Yoga, considered the province of cranks two decades ago, is now taught in most local council evening classes. Everywhere people are seeking to enrich their lives through the study of comparative religion, through the practice of meditation and by following a whole variety of spiritual disciplines and regimes to unfold their awareness. Eastern philosophy has permeated the West opening whole new vistas of knowledge to the general public. Housewives and business men who sought relaxation through hatha yoga stay on to learn the principles of meditation, and progress into raja yoga and the control of the mind, seeking to make it a suitable vehicle for spiritual impression of a higher nature. All of these factors will serve, if properly employed and utilized, to cleanse, purify and give resilience to the aura and by so doing offset the effects of many of the negative and destructive forces present in the world today.

To become aware of your aura and its qualities is to become self-aware. To learn and apply the techniques available for the purification of your aura is to bring light to your environment. The theme of light and transfiguration runs through all spiritual teachings. In the Bible it says, 'By their light ye shall know them' (see Matthew 5.16). The Iranian Sufi masters speak of escape, ascent and deliverance from the world of the personality with its suffering and pain, through a kind of alchemic sublimination of the divine luminescence held prisoner in the 'darkness' of the physical form. Just as in alchemy the precious metals rise to the surface, so the divine inner light radiates out from the body to form the *aura gloriae*. The vermilion-gold backgrounds of many old Persian manuscripts and Byzantine icons are symbolic, perhaps literal representations of this transforming light.

So often today people look at the world situation and feel resigned to the idea that there is nothing they can do, but the truth is that the power of the purified aura is immeasurable. To transform oneself is to transform the world — we can only begin where we are and with ourselves. As Don Juan tells Castaneda, the warrior does not whine, he accepts life and gets on with it, adopting a posture of alertness. There is an axiom in the world of computers which can be readily applied to the human aura: it is GI — GO which means Garbage In — Garbage Out. If you allow your aura to be filled with garbage, you will add your qualities to it as it circulates and then you will feed it back into the aura of the planet. On the other hand if you see to it that the transformative light in your aura is cultivated it will form a natural barrier to environmental garbage at all levels of the psyche, and you will feed that light into your world and according to its potency it will help others, particularly those with whom you come into daily contact.

Jesus said that when two or more are gathered in my name I will be there (see Matthew 18.20). It is a curious fact that when two or more people do pray or meditate together there is not just a doubling of power but a manifold increase, such is the effect of coming together with a common purpose in prayer. It is a fact as far as science is concerned that whenever two or more oscillators are pulsing at nearly the same time they tend to 'lock in' and synchronize, pulsing at exactly the same time. It has been observed that people in groups will unconsciously synchronize their breathing. Two women sharing living accommodation may find that their menstrual cycles will synchronize. In counselling situations the heartbeats of the patient and therapist may also synchronize, such is the powerful influence of the auric field. The Bible reports that wherever the disciple Peter walked, his shadow (aura) healed the sick. Jesus knew immediately when the woman with an issue of blood touched the hem of his robe (aura), and the virtue (energy) went out of him and healed her. When the aura has such transforming power as this, no physical action is necessary, it heals whatever it touches, provided the aura it touches has the capacity to respond. To a lesser degree we all have this ability, particularly if we fill our aura with the transforming power of love. When Jesus said that others would do what he had done, and even greater things, it was no idle statement. He knew that when people recognized the transforming radiance within them and applied it to the daily round of life, that the kingdom would appear on earth, that life would take on a whole new meaning and be an experience of joy rather than suffering. The aura as we shall see is a subject of vital and practical importance, particularly in the world of today and the current transitional crisis.

2

The vital force revisited

> Whatever you see in the universe, whatever moves or works
> or has life, is a manifestation of prana. The sum total of the
> energy displayed in the universe is called prana.
>
> *Raja Yoga* — Swami Vivekananda

Before considering more detailed descriptions of the
human aura, it is essential to have some understanding
of the vital force that permeates all physical forms, because this force is closely associated with our knowledge
of the aura. Priest-physicians and philosophers down
through the ages have taken care to point out that the
auric fields arise from the interaction of the life-force with
matter. What then is the life-force and how is it related to
the aura?

Different cultures and men of different persuasions and
outlook have given it various names, but all have agreed
in principle as to its qualities and characteristics. They see
it as a universally present cosmic energy, permeating all
space and interpenetrating every form therein. To all forms
it imparts life, vitality and coherency. In the ancient Vedas
of India it is called *prana* and has close associations with
the sun as the giver of life. In his book *The Philosophy of
The Upanishads*, Paul Deussen writes:

> Breathing, circulation of the blood, and nourishment equally with the quickening of the body are the functions of prana, which penetrates the whole body in its varieties as prana, apana, vyana, udana and samana. According to S'ankara, the prana causes exspiration, the apana inspiration. The vyana sustains life when the breath is arrested. The samana is concerned with digestion. The udana effects departure of the soul from the body at death.

Whilst this passage reflects the more mundane functions of prana, other passages speak of the worshipper who, through his meditation, identifies himself with prana, and in so doing comprehends all gods and reaches a state of indestructibility. The concept that man can reach a state of immortality through the right control of the life-force is to be found in many esoteric teachings. Considerable detail is given on the subject in the Wilhelm translation of the Chinese text known as *The Secret of the Golden Flower*, which deals with this inner alchemical process. According to the text there are various ways in which the force can be brought under control, and the adept has to learn to circulate this energy as light until he transforms himself from a mortal to one of the immortals.

Adepts, whether they are yogis, priests, sages, or shaman, have learned through meditation and spiritual exercises to control the life-force. It is said that the yogi who can control prana can move an atom or a planet at will, so awesome is its power. The ability to walk on water, to bilocate, to become invisible and to pass unhindered through solid objects is derived from the control of specific aspects of prana. Tibetan and Aboriginal shaman have the power to 'fast walk' gliding over the ground at speeds that enable them to outdistance a galloping horse. Control of the life-force enables people to walk through fire unscathed, and to perform a variety of feats we would consider almost miraculous. In an article entitled 'Wuradjeri Magic and "Clever Men"' written by R.M. Berndt, the author describes interviews with two older members of the Wuradjeri tribe of New South Wales. One of these men had been initiated in 1882 and he described a demonstration of magic at this ceremony by a shaman or 'clever man' whose name was Dagan. A huge fire was built at his instruction and he told the elders and initiates to sit around the fire and watch him. Dagan went away from the fire to the top of a slight rise and lay down full length. He then began to roll slowly towards the fire; he passed through the ring of people who made space for him and rolled right into the blaze. Once he was engulfed in the flames he proceeded to roll about making the sound 'fi: 'fi: 'fi: scattering hot coals in all directions. Finally he got up and walked out of the fire and stood with the others. The European clothes he wore were unharmed. Following this he went to the butt of a tree, lay on his back with his legs stretched apart and his hands by his side, and in this position with his head well back proceeded to climb forty feet or so to the top of the tree. The climb, according to the informant, was accomplished with the use of a magic cord which Dagan 'sang' out of his testes. He returned to the ground in the same position using the cord which then retracted into his body. Such exhibitions of magic were not uncommon at initiations, and were given in order to impress the initiates and novices. Berndt reports that one of the most popular forms of magical demonstration was that of walking through air, by the aid of a magic cord, from one tree to another, then disappearing and soon afterwards reappearing in another tree. Such demonstrations are to be found in the writings of Castaneda, who describes how *brujo* Don Genaro climbs across the face of a waterfall by means of tentacles issuing from his solar plexus, and similarly appearing and reappearing in different tree tops.

The Aborigine calls the life-force *kuranita*, and states

that all forms contain various amounts. Adult men, they say, possess more of this essence than women or children, and it is to be found in the rocks, water-courses, the trees, animals, the stars and planets and in the grasses, left there by the mythical men and women of the dreamtime known as the *tjukurita*. There are certain localities where the kuranita is highly concentrated, and it is at these places that special ceremonies are carried out to manipulate the life-force in such a way as to increase the local flora and fauna which serve as food in their incredibly harsh environment. As in all tribal societies blood is regarded as the main vehicle of the life-force, and, as elsewhere, it plays an important role in their ceremonies.

Such ceremonies take place at totemic centres known as *pulkarin*. Usually a special rock is struck with a stone held in the hand; the rock may well have been used for thousands of years for increase purposes and as such is a sanctified repository of a specific type of life-force. It may be the life-force of a particular bird, lizard, grub, plant, or seed, and it is used to increase the supply, not just for the tribe, but for all people. The rock is struck with a regular beat and an invocation is chanted in order to activate the life-force. This, according to the Aborigines, rises into the air like a fine mist whereupon it impregnates the particular tree or animal associated with it and brings about an increase.

Professor A.P. Elkin, in his book on the Aboriginal shaman entitled *Aboriginal Men of High Degree*, writes that they are able to diagnose disease with great accuracy by looking through the flesh to the organs within the body cavities. Disease may be described as colour; blackness of the heart and liver and areas of red, grey and white are outlined by them. When the belly cavity and the intestines are clear then the person has no sickness. Elkin also points out that they have a remarkable ability to look into another person's mind.

He is indeed able, once he can get en rapport with,
or visualize them, to ransack their mind — a process
termed telaesthesia, and not confined to ransacking
the mind as it is at the time of enquiry, but also as
it was in the past.

Like the Aborigines the Polynesians of the Pacific
Islands were familiar with the life-force. They called
it *manas*, which sounds very similar to the manna of the
Bible. The Polynesians and in particular the Kuhuna
priests of Hawaii were reputed to be able to use the life-
force in a number of ways. Max Freedom Long in his
book *The Secret Science behind the Miracles*, described
how they performed instant healing with manas, demonstrated control over sharks and the weather, walked bare-
foot over slightly solidified larva, foretold the future and
where necessary altered the outcome of events to the
advantage of the tribe. It would appear that the ability to
control the life-force bestows a similarity of gifts on
people many thousands of miles apart, thus indicating
its universality.

As an old civilization the Chinese have delved deeply
into the secrets of the vital force; they call it *chi*. This
energy plays a paramount role in the treatment of disease
in China, and in fact throughout the world. In the ancient
healing art of acupuncture which originated there, needles
are placed at specific points along energy pathways in the
body known as meridians. Correct placement and manipulation of the needles within the flow of chi that courses
along the meridians restores balance to the flow and this
in turn promotes health and cures disease. So remarkable
is this concept to the Western mind that acupuncture was
derided by science and medicine in particular, until recent
times when it was repeatedly used to demonstrate its
capacity to anaesthetize patients for major surgery. Opera-
tions were carried out with the patient fully conscious
and feeling no pain, nor suffering from post-operative

shock as is often the case in Western medicine.

In *The Yellow Emperor's Classic of Internal Medicine*, the sage physician Ch'i Po is speaking to the Emperor about the life-force and colour, and he says: 'The colour of life displayed by the heart is like the vermilion red lining of a white silk robe; the colour of life displayed by the lungs is like the lucky red lining of a white silk robe.' And elsewhere in the same text: 'When the viscera are green like the kingfisher's wings they are full of life, when they are red like a cock's comb they are full of life.' There can be little doubt that the colours seen by the sages and shaman of old are those which ultimately reflect into the aura and surround the human form with light. Like the Chinese sages, the seers of India psychically observed the life-force and described it in terms of colour. In the Chandogya Upanishad there is a beautiful passage which to my mind is so descriptive that it could well serve as a seed thought for meditation:

> Orange, blue, yellow, red, are not less in a man's arteries than in the sun. As a long highway passes between two villages, one at either end, so the sun's rays pass between this world and the world beyond. They flow from the sun, enter into the arteries, flow back from the arteries, enter into the sun.

Here the direct relationship between the life-force and the sun is depicted. We should be aware however that where the word artery is used in this context, it usually refers to the *nadis* which are the fibres of light and energy that make up the subtle nervous system and the etheric body.

As we have already seen the sages divided prana into a number of categories, which when consciously controlled conferred various *siddhis* or occult powers. In broad terms however there are three divisions. First, solar prana, which they described as a vital magnetic force that radiates from the sun and passes into the human etheric body by way of certain vortices of energy known as *chakras*. The word chakra is Sanskrit for wheel or circle, and these vortices have a circular, whirling appearance as they draw various forces and energies into the body. Prana is taken in and distributed throughout the etheric body via the spleen, in order to vitalize the physical form and maintain it in a state of health. Secondly there is planetary prana, the vital energy emanating from the earth itself. In effect it is solar prana that has been drawn into the etheric body of the earth, circulated and radiated from the surface, carrying its own distinctive quality outwards to form a part of earth's aura. This is sometimes spoken of as the magnetism of Mother Earth. Thirdly there is the prana of forms which consists of solar and planetary prana that has been used by the vegetable, animal, mineral and human kingdom and is then transmitted by surface radiation.

Even modern man, despite the dulling or atrophy of his sensitivity, is aware that there are areas and locations where he feels better. At the beach for example there are high energy levels present: sand, it seems, in some way or other can store large amounts of prana, and the ocean itself carries a high charge of these forces. When we are jaded and our nervous systems on edge there is nothing like a day on some isolated sunny beach to restore the balance. Forests too are reservoirs of the life-force, and both pine and eucalyptus trees have a reputation for being able to impart vitality to those who stay in close proximity to them. High mountain areas also carry potent amounts of prana, which gives that clear sparkling quality to the atmosphere. For this reason spas and sanatoriums are frequently located on mountain slopes and forests, because patients will recover more rapidly under such conditions.

The prana of forms comes to us very directly through our food, especially in the form of fruits, fresh vegetables, nuts and honey. Absorption of prana begins in the mouth, hence the importance of chewing food well before swallowing. Clearly it is an advantage to have organically grown products if at all possible, in order to avoid insecticide and herbicide residues, and to have a product that is chock-full of prana. People today are demanding such foods because there is a growing recognition of their importance to health. The same goes for the vitamins we supplement our meals with: they should be from natural sources. The scientist will tell you that the molecular structure of synthetic vitamin C is no different from natural vitamin C, and he is right in his terms; what he misses however is the essential life-force that only the natural product can contain. Science does not recognize this force, so it cannot exist, much less have any importance, as far as they are concerned. Junk foods are of course the very antithesis of fresh unprocessed foods, and serve only to clog the etheric and physical bodies with devitalized material that is often harmful to health.

As we breathe we take in prana which is absorbed at the back of the nostrils into the etheric body. Habitual mouth breathers are often vacuous and usually of low intelligence, which points to the importance of keeping the nasal passages clear and breathing properly. The yogis of India long ago perfected the art of breathing and developed an entire system of exercise known as *pranayama*. With care these can be employed to enhance the vitality of the etheric body and improve health.

It is clear that the sages, seers and 'clever men' who were masters of the life-force accepted it as a demonstrable reality. Just how far back their knowledge goes we cannot tell, but the Aboriginal has a history of some forty to fifty thousand years on the Australian continent, and the Bushmen of Africa a similar period of time during which they have worked with this force in magical and practical ways. Knowledge of the force has enabled them to survive and indeed flourish for thousands of years, in environments that would kill off a mechanistic behaviourist in a few days. From the continent of India and from the civilizations of the Far East have come philosophies and systems of religious thought that are, in many of their aspects, woven around the central theme of a life-force. This type of vitalist approach survived in the West until fairly recently, and as it declined and modern science and technology replaced it, a great change began to manifest which has brought about a destruction and exploitation of natural resources on an unprecedented scale. One cannot help feeling that sooner or later there will be a catastrophic backlash, and Nature will restore the balance.

Our record of exploring the life-force pales into insignificance besides the efforts of ancient man. Not that there has been much encouragement; quite the opposite in fact. Over the past two hundred years or so, four men of outstanding genius have trodden this rocky path. All were persecuted in one way or another, all were ridiculed by their peers. Two were prosecuted under law and one of them was hauled into court on the basis that the life-force did not exist, and subsequently died in gaol for his efforts. The Establishment it seems does not look kindly on those who seek to explore these energies, and as we shall see later, the evidence suggests that there is an active campaign against them in one form or another.

The four brave souls who put their reputations on the line were a rather mixed bunch, born in a cluster over a period of about one hundred years. Three of them in fact were alive and researching at the same time, and were therefore aware to a great extent of each other's work. Their names are:

Baron Karl von Reichenbach   Born 1788, died 1869
Dr Edwin Babbitt   Born 1829, died 1905
John Keely   Born 1837, died 1898
Dr Wilhelm Reich   Born 1897, died 1957

Baron von Reichenbach was a brilliant industrialist and chemist, the discoverer of paraffin and creosote, a metallurgist and an expert on meteorites. Von Reichenbach's father was the court librarian in Stuttgart, and Karl was educated in the local high school and later at the State University of Tübingen where he studied natural science and political economy. Despite such interruptions to his studies as being gaoled for setting up a secret society to establish the German Reich in the South Sea Islands, von Reichenbach graduated with a degree of Ph.D. and a keen interest in the philosophical aspects of life. He travelled extensively over France and Germany looking into the construction and commercial utilization of ironworks. By 1825 he was something of a magnate with estates, blast furnaces and steel works in various parts of Austria and Germany. Despite the success of such commercial ventures, von Reichenbach was busy experimenting in his laboratories delving into the mysteries of electricity and magnetism. These held his attention so firmly that he withdrew to a great extent from business affairs and concentrated on the researches that eventually made his name so famous.

Von Reichenbach became fascinated with the vital force which he called the odylic force or Od for short. He describes how he arrived at this name in his book *The Odic Force*.

I have considered myself called upon to make use of this property of exemption from all obstructibility, in order to form a convenient name for it, pliable enough to adapt itself to the multifarious needs of science. 'Va' in Sanskrit means 'to move about'. 'Vado' in Latin and 'vada' in old Norse means 'I go quickly, hurry away, stream forth'. Hence 'Wodan' in old Germanic expresses the idea of the 'All transcending'; in the various old idioms it appears as 'Woudan', 'Odan', and ultimately personified as a Germanic deity. 'Od' is consequently the word to express a dynamid of force which, with a power that cannot be obstructed, quickly penetrates and courses through everything in the universe.

While this is a rather long-winded explanation of how he came to name the life-force, it does show that he knew something of the origins of the principle he was dealing with, and its universal nature. In order to make observations of the odic force, von Reichenbach used the services of many sensitives and clairvoyants. In the course of his studies he worked with some two hundred of these people who could clairvoyantly see the odic energies, and it should be mentioned that over one hundred of them had scientific backgrounds — at least fifty were physicians, chemists, physicists, mathematicians, or philosophers. This being the case it can be assumed that their reports with respect to what they observed should contain a high degree of accuracy and objectivity.

Von Reichenbach and his sensitives worked with a variety of objects in order to observe the odic force. Magnets, for example, were commonly used. To clairvoyant sight they gave off a particularly bright light at their poles, the north being surrounded by a white light merging into layers of red, yellow, green and finally blue. The middle of the magnet gave off a glowing green haze, and the south pole an even brighter white than the north, merging into red. If lengths of wire were exposed outdoors to sunshine, the odic energy ran along the wire into the laboratories and appeared as flame-like emanations from the other end. This energy was also observed to surround the human body, and flow from the finger tips of people. Of the human aura von Reichenbach wrote:

> In somewhat shaded light, say in a room where the brilliancy of day has become enfeebled by the sky being overcast, or in evening candlelight, let a man hold his hand before his eyes at ordinary seeing distance. Then let him look at his finger tips, holding them against a dark background distant a step or two. Most men will see nothing unusual under such cir-

cumstances. But there will be a few among them everywhere who make an exception. These, on their attention
being drawn to the matter, will by looking narrowly,
make out over the tip of each finger an extremely
delicate current, colourless, non-luminous, like air,
subject to motion.

What von Reichenbach outlines for us here is a simple
exercise that anyone who wishes to begin to develop
sensitivity to auric emanations can carry out. The colourless energy, looking very much like warm currents of air
rising from a hot surface on a summer's day, is in all
probability the coarser part of the aura, and thus easier
to see. With a little more perceptive ability this tenuous
haze takes on the appearance of a band of greyish-blue
light about a half to one inch wide that surrounds the
entire physical form.

In his studies, von Reichenbach was impressed that all
forms gave off a luminosity, and this clearly excited his
imagination because he was aware, as we should be, of the
philosophical and spiritual implications inherent in this
fact. He wrote: 'Everything, then, emits light; everything,
everything! We live in a world full of shining matter. . . .
Well, is this luminosity odic? It is because it has all the
characteristics of od.' He goes on to say very much what
the ancient sages and tribal shaman have given voice to
in the hymns and esoteric lore of their traditions.

Od, therefore, not only flows in concentrated form
from special sources, but is, in addition, a general
endowment of the whole of Nature, a variously shared
but universally distributed natural force, such as heat,
electricity, chemical affinity, gravity, etc. It interpenetrates and fills the structure of the universe, present
in the smallest things as well as the greatest.

At the time von Reichenbach was carrying out his
work in Europe, Dr Edwin Babbitt was involved in his own

investigations of the life-force in the United States. Babbitt was aware of von Reichenbach's experiments, and had an advantage in some respects in that he himself was clairvoyant and could make his observations first hand. Babbitt was in fact an odd combination of artist, mystic and physician, with a wide and intensive education. He had a reputation as a miracle man for his healing work with colour, and even today his book *The Principles of Light and Color* is a classic.

In his healing work Babbitt deliberately utilized the pranic energies to increase the efficacy of each colour. For example he stood specially constructed coloured glass flasks in full sunlight in order that the water they contained could pick up a strong charge of energy. He designed a colour therapy instrument called the Chromolume which consisted of a complex glass frame containing various shapes and sizes of coloured glass. This frame was hung in front of a window so that light shone through the colours onto the patient who sat in front of it. These Chromolume frames were all custom built to treat the individual patient, and Babbitt enjoyed a wide reputation due to his success with these methods.

Babbitt made many observations of the human aura and the energies present in the environment. He describes his viewing of subtle energies and colours in poetic language.

Sometimes fountains of light would pour towards me from luminous centers merging into all the iridescent splendours on their way. Sometimes radiations would flow out from me and become lost to view in the distance. More generally flashing streams of light would move to and fro in straight lines, though sometimes fluidic emanations would sweep around in the curves of a parabola as in a fountain. What was more marvellous than almost anything else was the infinite millions of radiations, emanations and luminous currents which at times I would see streaming from and into and through all things, and filling all the surrounding space with coruscations and lightning activities.

Both von Reichenbach and Babbitt made substantial contributions to our knowledge of the life-force through experimentation, observation and practical application. Both were derided by their peer groups, but neither seemed to suffer anything more than a sense of frustration from these attacks. John Keely and Wilhelm Reich on the other hand fared very badly at the hands of the law, because of the adverse publicity given to their investigations. Both seemed more vulnerable to attack, and curiously enough both penetrated into the mysterious powers of the life-force to discover a motor force. Keely attempted to exploit his discovery, while Reich, cognizant of the unlimited destructive power it contained, never committed anything to paper, and his secrets died with him.

John Keely, born in 1837, was a contemporary of Babbitt. His work was based on a theory that the atmosphere contained countless units of energy, which he called cosmic corpuscles. Using his own complex theory of harmonics he demonstrated that these corpuscles could be divided by vibrations to produce a motor force out of thin air. This power became known as the Dynaspheric Force. In fact Keely coined all manner of strange names for this force, among them Vibro-Molecular, Vibro-Atomic and Sympathetic Vibro-Etheric Forces.

Keely eventually demonstrated this force to a group of business men who were sufficiently impressed to raise $5 million in five years to back his work. In those days it was a massive sum of money, but Keely was clearly onto something unusual and the business men were quick to recognize the potential of his discoveries, and the commercial possibilities. Under the auspices of the Keely Motor Company, Keely intensified his research and sought to produce for his backers a commercial motor that would run on the Dynaspheric Force.

Keely's work is documented in a book entitled *Keely and his Discoveries*, by Clara Bloomfield Moore, who for many years encouraged him in his research and supported him financially. He produced some remarkable inventions with even more remarkable names that had a science fiction ring to them, for example there was the Compound Disintegrator, the Provisional Motor, the Musical Ball, the Globe Engine, a Vibratory Accumulator and a Pneumatic Rocket Gun. Strange as these names may seem, Keely did in fact give some outstanding demonstrations of the Dynaspheric Force. With a note played on a violin he could set this energy in motion and fly a model Zeppelin weighing eight pounds around the room, moving it where he wanted it to go and making it hover. Even more impressive was the fact that he could start and run a twenty-five horsepower electric motor in the same manner, until it reached such a speed that it almost shook from its moorings. The motor needless to say was not attached to any electrical source. Enough of the Dynaspheric Force could be harnessed to turn a seventy-two pound pulley wheel, and to float a solid iron ball on water. It is little wonder that his backers were impressed, because Keely was on to something, something even he did not fully comprehend.

Keely worked day and night in his efforts to produce a commercial motor. On more than one occasion the forces that he unleashed nearly blew him and his laboratories to pieces. Mounting problems dogged his efforts and Keely was frustrated again and again — he knew beyond any shadow of a doubt that his discovery was one of the most remarkable ever made, he knew that success was right there waiting for him, but always some intangible and indefinable influence blocked the way. His backers became more and more demanding but finally their patience and money ran out. Keely tried to explain that he was right on the verge of a breakthrough but they had heard all this before. Demands were made that he hand over the work he had accomplished, and make available his experimental and research notes. Eventually he was gaoled for contempt of court for refusing to hand over his secrets to a committee that had been set up to judge the validity of his work.

Even if the committee had gone through his material, it is doubtful if they would have understood what lay before them. Keely himself was the X factor in the unleashing of the Dynaspheric Force. Without him it would not have worked, unless he finally succeeded in externalizing that principle within him, in the form of a mechanical device. The motor of course was never produced, and Keely died a disillusioned and a very puzzled man in 1898.

There is an interesting sequel to Keely's story, which takes the form of rumours and occasionally articles. These rumours and articles state that there are individuals who have followed up Keely's work and rediscovered the principles he worked with, and where he failed they have succeeded. One article described an Italian gentleman who no longer has to pay power bills because he has discovered how to pull energy out of the atmosphere and uses it to heat and light his home. In these days of soaring gas and electricity bills this is a story to catch the imagination. On the other hand it may simply be an urban myth. Irrespective of this the fact is that once man has unlocked the secrets of the ethers, as Keely had begun to, it will be possible to gain access to unlimited energy for heating, lighting and for transportation purposes. Of course free energy on that scale may be seen as something of a threat to those with vested interests, and might be met by considerable resistance.

Wilhelm Reich met resistance. He was born in Austria in 1897, studied at the University of Vienna and graduated in 1922. Later he did postgraduate work in neuro-psychiatry. An outspoken man with perceptive if unusual ideas, a man who did not suffer fools gladly, Reich found himself being harassed by certain professional and political factions in Europe during the 1930s. Eventually he moved to the United States where he felt he would have a better opportunity and more freedom to work as he pleased.

In the course of his work in the psychiatric field Reich discovered what he called orgone energy, which he claimed vitalized every living thing, and which was in fact a universal life-force. Reich observed that this energy surrounded plants, minerals, animals, birds, people and in fact all life forms. He called this surround an 'orgone envelope' and developed a simple telescope-like instrument called an Orgonescope to observe this energy. Reich's description of the orgone energy and its properties differ little, if at all, from the descriptions given by the Vedic seers of India thousands of years ago, or by Reichenbach, Babbitt and Keely. Orgone by any other name is chi, prana, od or dynaspheric force, they are all one and the same energy. Reich never acknowledged this fact, although he must have been well aware of it; rather he tended to sneer at mysticism whenever the opportunity arose.

Through observation and experimentation Reich found that orgone energy could be concentrated in large amounts in boxes made up of alternating layers of organic and inorganic materials. When such a box was stood outdoors in sub-zero temperatures, the temperature inside the box was significantly higher than the external one. If you built such a box large enough to sit in, you could acquire a sun tan without going out in the sun. Reich found that if the energy from the accumulators was directed onto cuts, burns or other injuries with a tube known as a 'shooter', rapid healing was initiated with sometimes instantaneous reduction of pain. Reich observed that in general when people were dis-eased, their tensions set themselves into various muscle groups — he called this character armour. This armour reflected a stasis of the orgone energy field of the patient, and brought about a certain rigidity of mind and body. He found this to be particularly true of cancer patients and sought to help them through counselling and the use of the orgone accumulator. It was this and his penchant for attacking the orthodoxy of the day that finally led to his prosecution.

Reich's experiments were not confined to medicine entirely, and his wide ranging ideas brought him into other areas of exploration. He was interested in the connection between weather patterns and orgone energy, and this interest led to the development of an instrument consisting of a battery of long tubes called a Cloudbuster. With the Cloudbuster, Reich began to experiment in the Arizona desert. By setting up the device near a source of water and pointing the tubes at a sky devoid of clouds, Reich actually succeeded in forming sufficient clouds in the area to precipitate rainfall. He called this work cosmic orgone engineering.

Research was also carried out in order to observe the interactions between orgone energy and radioactive material. The upshot of this work proved almost disastrous: the normal background level of radioactivity rose sharply in an area of many square miles around the laboratory, and proved to be so persistent that Reich stopped his experiments, and eventually had to dismantle the entire building that the work had been carried out in. In the process of this dismantling an assistant who poked her head into a cabinet was rendered senseless and had great difficulty in breathing.

Reich discovered many things about orgone energy. A lot of his information is common knowledge today. What he did not reveal to anyone was information in respect to the motor force. Like Keely he had found the key to unlimited power, but so frightening were the implications that he never committed any of this knowledge to paper, nor shared it with any of his fellow workers. Reich said that if this secret was to fall into the hands of any government agency it could well spell death for the human race. When we once again consider the Vedic statement, that a yogi who has full control of prana can move an atom or a planet at will, it may well be that Reich was correct in letting his secrets die with him.

With all of the controversy that surrounded his work, Reich finally fell foul of the law. He was summoned to court on a charge so insignificant that he did not bother to turn up to answer it. The outcome of this was a further summons and a charge of contempt of court, and he was given a gaol sentence of two years for the contempt. Reich was forced to close down his laboratories and stand by and watch as the local sheriff with an axe proceeded to smash his equipment and destroy a lifetime's work. Subsequently Reich's research papers and books were burned and his writings banned from publication. Determined to humiliate him to the full, prison authorities even denied him pencil and paper in his cell. Reich was convinced that the authorities would not allow him to survive, and although it was reported that he died of natural causes in gaol, one cannot help but wonder if Reich's premonition became a fact.

I find it curious and wonder just why it was that these four pioneers ran into so much resistance. Baron von Reichenbach and Dr Edwin Babbitt did not fare badly, but then their work hardly skimmed the surface of this vast subject. For von Reichenbach it was a subject that excited his fertile imagination and curiosity, and Babbitt hardly made an issue of this energy but went about his practice of colour healing. Keely and Reich on the other hand had penetrated deeply into the mystery, they were visibly manipulating the life-force in quite remarkable ways, and had their researches continued they may well have threatened vested interests and radically upset the current beliefs of science. No doubt the Establishment saw them as dangerous men and acted accordingly, but there may have been another angle to this; they were after all experimenting with a force of unlimited potential. We jokingly speak of higher intervention as though it is nothing more than a myth, but I wonder.

The theosophist, Madame Blavatsky, certainly was of the opinion that Keely was frustrated and thwarted in his work by Higher Powers, and for the reason that man was not as yet ready for the deeper secrets of the life-force, and incapable of handling the power in a constructive manner. She did in fact write something on the subject which confirms that Keely unwittingly got in too deep for the safety of humanity, and had to be gently prevented from succeeding. No wonder he died a puzzled man — he knew that he had the answer, but some invisible hand held him back, blocking the outcome of years of unique and outstanding work. It must be a peculiar feeling to hold the key to a universal secret of that magnitude, and every time you go to put it in the lock, the keyhole seems to dissolve. Blavatsky's opinion was recorded in the following words:

> If the question is asked why Mr. Keely was not allowed to pass a certain limit, the answer is easy; it was because what he had discovered was the terrible sidereal Force known to, and named by, the Atlanteans Mash-Mak and by the Aryan Rishis in their Astra Vidya by a name we do not care to give. It is the Vril of Bulwer Lytton's Coming Race and of the coming races of our mankind. The name Vril may be a fiction; the Force itself is a fact, since it is mentioned in all the secret books. . . once in the hands of a modern Attilla, [it] would in a few days reduce Europe to its primitive chaotic state, with no man alive to tell the tale — is it this Force which is to become the common property of all men alike?

Clearly the answer to Madame Blavatsky's question is no! Man is not ready to handle the secrets of such a Force creatively. In the present climate of political and social unrest, it would be turned immediately towards destructive purposes.

Our limited knowledge, then, is in effect a blessing, and despite the fact that we have lost our ability to manipulate the life-force with the skill of a tribal shaman, we can still put our knowledge to use. How? Well, by first of all recognizing the existence of this energy, by becoming conscious of it and making sure that our life styles enhance its qualities. This is done quite simply by eating fresh vital foods, getting plenty of fresh water, fresh air, sunshine and exercise. These in turn will help to cleanse and enhance the aura, thus providing a basis for physical and inner harmony.

3

Subtle bodies, chakras and the aura

> The pilgrim rising from one degree to another discovers
> on each higher level a subtler state, a more entrancing
> beauty, a more intense spirituality, a more overflowing
> delight.
>
> *Spiritual Body and Celestial Earth* — Henry Corbin

All esoteric spiritual teachings refer to a hierarchy of
substance and consciousness, in fact no distinction is
made between the two. Blavatsky in her writings declared
that matter was spirit in its lowest expression, and that
spirit was matter in its highest. In common with many
other schools of thought, theosophy teaches that there
are seven planes or levels of consciousness, each of which
are divided into seven sub-planes. The Sufi teachers refer
to these levels as heavens, and Corbin writes of the seven
'handfuls of Heaven' and the seven 'handfuls of Earth'
which have their mutual correspondences in man. Psychic
constructs or maps of consciousness have emerged down
the ages from various spiritual disciplines, and their purpose is to guide the seeker on his explorations of inner
space. The mystics make frequent references to a spiritual
geography, and describe in detail countries, cities, land-
scapes, houses, palaces, deserts, rivers and mountains.

Bunyan's *The Pilgrim's Progress* is one such map that many of us are familiar with, and like the rest it provides signposts and descriptions of places and experiences, which seekers will recognize as they come to them along their own spiritual path. It is important to keep in mind that the map is not the terrain itself, and that the deserts and rivers are metaphors for states of consciousness and conditions to be confronted on the inner way.

The Sufi shayks speak of the subtle organism of man as being buried beneath a mountain, and they provide a detailed description for the traveller on his upward journey into the light of spiritual awareness. Colours, they tell him, will appear as indications of progress. Greens, yellows and blues are seen — green being the colour of the life of the heart, the sign of vitality and spiritual energy, signifying the power to actualize. Any dimness of colours will indicate fatigue and affliction arising from the battle with the lower-self, whose colour is blue. A Sufi text says: 'Without interruption you will see lights rising and light descending. The flames of the fire are all around you — very pure, very ardent, and very strong.' Sufi mystics are frequently portrayed with an aura of flames pouring from their bodies and pointing upwards, thus revealing the purity and clarity of their consciousness. In his book, *The Man of Light in Iranian Sufism*, Henry Corbin writes: 'And then all the spiritual Heavens, the inner Heavens of the soul, the seven planes of being which have their counterparts in the man of light shine multicoloured in the rainbow of the visio smaragdina.'

Wherever we look in spiritual literature we will find references to light and colour with respect to the inner nature of man. The Biblical story of Joseph with his coat of many colours is one such example. Joseph's coat is a metaphor for his aura, and the colours are the radiant energies he has brought out into his aura. So outstanding was his 'coat' that it led to jealousy and he was sold into bondage, no doubt another metaphor for the beginning of a new aspect of his inner journey.

As Edgar Cayce says, an aura is an effect, not a cause. What then lies behind the aura, from where or what does it radiate? Logically if auras are seen to surround forms, then there must be some kind of subtle form or body that gives rise to the various components of the aura. The levels of consciousness we spoke of earlier give us a clue to these forms, and the fact that the aura reflects physical, emotional and mental phenomena in terms of light and colour indicates that we have bodies from which these activities arise. It is said that man does in fact have a vehicle or body of manifestation on each of the seven major levels of consciousness, but for purposes of aura study we do not have to go too deeply into this at the initial stages. It suffices to say that in broad terms man is spirit, soul and body, or high-, middle- and low-self. Our primary concern is the low-self with its various divisions, for it is from these divisions or bodies that the aura arises.

Various teachings differ as to these divisions, but the consensus of opinion is that the lower-self, or personality as it is often called, has four aspects to it. They are first, the dense physical body, secondly the etheric or vital bioplasmic body, thirdly the emotional body which is often referred to as the astral body, and finally the mental body or vehicle of the mind. It will help I think to give brief details of this 'city which stands foursquare' under a series of headings beginning from the bottom and working upwards.

THE PHYSICAL BODY

The dense physical body is the lowest aspect of our form life. In its divisions we see a reflection of the inner levels of consciousness. In some texts it is called the body temple and we see that it does indeed have three divisions of a temple of worship. First the abdominal cavity, the outer court of the temple containing the organs of assimilation and procreation, reflecting functions of the more mundane world. Above this is the great dividing barrier of the diaphragm, representing a veil between higher and lower levels of consciousness. The chest cavity symbolizes the inner court of the temple, containing the organs of the heart and lungs whose function it is to bring the life-force into circulation. While the abdominal cavity symbolizes the body, the chest cavity symbolizes the soul. Across the narrow bridge of the neck lies the head, or the holy of holies in the temple, the dwelling place of the spirit. Here we find the organs of spiritual perception, the pituitary and pineal glands. So we are, as Paul states, a temple of the living God. Every organ and every function is a symbol or metaphor for deep and complex spiritual truths. Little wonder that the Delphic oracle said: Man know thyself and thou wilt know God and the Universe.

THE ETHERIC BODY

Between spirit and body lies the soul, and between the physical body and its world, and the subtler emotional and mental bodies and their worlds, lies the etheric body. Symbol of the soul and a body of light, it is like the soul a mediating, vitalizing body. The Bible calls it 'The Golden Bowl' and in the fullness of time it does indeed radiate a golden hued stream of light into the darkness of the physical realm. The etheric body is the framework upon which the physical form is built, it is a transmitter of energies to the physical body which it vitalizes with prana. There are seven major spinal chakras within the etheric body; through these the interplay of various energies build and sustain our endocrine glands and the nervous system, and galvanize our organ systems into activity. I will deal with these chakras or centres in more detail a little further on. One other chakra of major importance in the etheric body is the spleen. It is through this centre that the etheric body receives and distributes prana, and this in turn energizes the physical form. The five senses work through the etheric body enabling the individual to function in time and space at the physical level. The etheric body is in reality the field where spiritual and physical worlds meet. It gives rise to what is commonly called the health aura, that rather narrow band of energy that hugs the physical form.

THE EMOTIONAL BODY

The emotional body as the term implies is that subtle form in which the interplay of emotional energies takes place. The alchemists called it the astral body because to inner sight it has a sparkling appearance if not clouded by negative emotions. In this body we experience the pull of opposites, happiness and depression, calmness and anger. It is our own personal heaven or hell in which we fight out the battle between the pulls of this world and those of the spiritual. Selfish desire and fear, excessive temper and irritation throw the astral body into feverish activity, with consequent effects upon the etheric body which result in fatigue and eventually organic lesions in the physical form. The symbol of the astral body is water, and were we able to calm the astral body like a lake on a windless day, then its surface would reflect deeper inner truths and a sense of tranquillity. We have two metaphors here which are of interest: water for the astral body and air for the mental. The mental and astral bodies interact as readily as wind upon water, one feeding the other. The Biblical story of Jesus walking on the water and rebuking the storm is nothing less than a demonstration to us of his control over the mental and astral aspects of his nature.

The Bible is full of such metaphors which unfortunately have been taken all too literally. It is comforting however to have been reassured that we shall do these things, and greater ones. Today the bulk of humanity are focused in their astral bodies and subject to all of the emotional ups and downs this brings with it. The disciplines of meditation and prayer are designed to overcome the forces of the astral plane and extract the seeker from the storms that sweep through this area of consciousness.

The astral aura tends to be ovoid in shape and stands out from the physical form for a distance of twelve to eighteen inches. It presents itself to clairvoyant sight as a field of interweaving colours. If the person concerned has conflicting emotional feelings then these colours will be harsh, chaotic and possibly muddy in appearance. The astral body from which this aura emanates is frequently referred to as the astral double. This is the body through which out of the body experiences, better known as OOBEs, take place. In moments of great physical stress, or under anaesthetic, and even in the dream state whilst sleeping or the moment of death, a person may appear in what looks like their physical form, and stand before a friend or relative, signifying their need for help or to inform someone of their death. Carl Jung recalls an experience like this in his autobiography, *Memories, Dreams, Reflections*, in which his old friend Wilhelm suddenly appeared one night at the foot of his bed, clad in a blue silk robe. As he faded from sight, Jung knew that his friend was dead. Many people have had the experience of passing out and suddenly finding themselves viewing their physical body from above. In such instances involving hospital emergencies, they can repeat verbatim what the doctors and nurses said, and describe their actions in detail. Return to the body is often sudden and results in an unconscious state until they recover once again.

THE MENTAL BODY

Theosophists posit a number of divisions to the mind or mental body. First the lower concrete mind, which is the reasoning principle that applies logic and common sense. It is the repository of acquired knowledge and the ability to discriminate. If it gets too active it throws the astral body into a state of activity. Too many negative and habitual thought patterns in the lower mind can pollute the astral body. It has separative tendencies, and in some ancient texts is referred to as the 'Slayer of the Real'; in other words it lords it over the emotional and etheric bodies to such an extent that little, if any, light or truth can enter from the intuitive mind.

Another aspect of the mental body is the higher abstract mind, the conveyor of spiritual truths and a reflector of divine love. Here repose the intuitive faculties and the capacity for pure reason.

The mental aura is seen as an ovoid form. In his book *Man — Grand Symbol of the Mysteries*, Manly Palmer Hall describes the relationship between this ovoid and the Cosmic Egg.

> From the Greek accounts we learn that the Cosmic Egg was also called in the language of the Mysteries, 'brilliant chiton' or 'the cloud.' The Macrocosmic Egg with its hypothetical boundaries, and the Microcosmic Egg is the human aura, the brilliant cloud in which man lives and moves and has his being.

When viewed by a clairvoyant the mental aura appears as a cloud of rapidly moving particles. Thought processes throw this field into activity, and manifest as patterns known as thought-forms. These circulate within the ovoid, expressing themselves in a variety of colours. Negative thoughts, hatred, prejudice, selfishness and greed create forms that by their very nature tend to accumulate in the lower part of the aura, and display themselves in coarse,

Figure 3.1 The large ovoid field of energy around the head and shoulders is a manifestation of psychic energy

dull colours. Higher thoughts on the other hand move to the upper part of the aura and are seen as bright, clear colours that are radiant and alive.

Muddled and unclear thinking can give rise to a sluggish aura, and the person whose thoughts are predominantly coarse will create an ovoid field with the larger part at the bottom, looking rather like a pear-shape. On the other hand a refined, intellectually clear-minded individual, who thinks with precision, will of course reverse this picture and have the larger circumference at the top of the aura. Thoughts, as they flash into colours and geometric forms, can be picked up by the skilled clairvoyant, and can be interpreted in such a way as to reveal the character of the person. Curiously enough, even without clairvoyance it is possible to register these colours and patterns in a general sense. It is something we do quite unconsciously all of the time. It is from these signals that we form our impressions of other people, and even of places. When you rapidly size someone up as being as 'dull as ditchwater' you have made that assessment on the colours of their mental aura, which no doubt fit the description. Dull people have dull auras, with muddy colours and indistinct thought-forms circulating around them. Another person will impress you, even across a room, as being sharp and vital; often just to physical sight they radiate clarity and a sense of purpose. When this is the impression you have of that person then you can be sure that their aura is filled with clear colours and precise, vital thought-forms.

Blue in the mental aura is equated with high spirituality, religious feeling and devotion to high ideals. Clear yellows and oranges indicate the highest forms of intellect. Whenever these colours are dull or mixed in with other dark shades, then this is an indication that clarity of thought and purpose has been lost. Good thoughts produce a fine mental aura; this simple truth lies at the heart of all spiritual disciplines. Through meditation and prayer we can learn to still the mind, to quieten the constant mental babble that goes on in our heads — the 'roof brain chatter' as Chilton Pearce calls it in his book, *The Crack in the Cosmic Egg.* This 'roof brain chatter' churns the mental aura into a confused mass of mixed colours and indistinct thought-forms. As we have to view the world through our own auras, these frantic patterns are going to distort our perception, and we may find that we are projecting these thoughts on to people and events, and possibly the world at large, thus adding to our problems. In view of this, it is easy to appreciate the Buddhist practice of right thought. To clarify our thinking processes is one of the first steps along the path to achieving liberation from the activities of our lower mind. We live in an age of left brain hemisphere dominance, where rational processes, logic and the intellect are gods. These tend to crush out the intuitive, transcendent and holistic functions of the right brain hemisphere. I cannot help feeling that there is a parallel between the left brain hemisphere and the carnal mind that St. Paul speaks of in the Bible and the lower-mind of theosophy. If this is the case then the right brain hemisphere may well equate with the abstract or higher-mind, which Paul referred to as the 'mind in Christ', which reflects the divine nature through love, understanding and inclusiveness.

Scientific research into brain hemisphere function, whilst becoming more holistic over the past few years, particularly through the work of American Roger Sperry, who shared the 1981 Nobel Prize in medicine and physiology, still categorically denies any connection between the current wider view of brain hemisphere function and mysticism or animism. Yet it is a curious fact that many scientists, whilst denying the mystical elements emerging from their work, are sounding more and more like Eastern sages in their proclamations.

In 1905 Annie Besant and C.W. Leadbeater wrote a book called *Thought-Forms* which describes and illustrates the variety of colours and patterns to be seen in the aura. They give a rather lovely description of the mental aura which bears repeating.

> It is an object of great beauty, the delicacy and rapid motion of its particles giving it an aspect of living iridescent light, and this beauty becomes an extra-ordinary radiant and entrancing loveliness as the intellect becomes more highly evolved and is employed chiefly on pure and sublime topics. As we shall see in detail later, every thought gives rise to vibrations in the mental body, accompanied by a play of colour described as like that of the spray of a waterfall as the sunlight strikes it, raised many degrees in colour and vivid delicacy.

The four-fold lower-self of man, then, has a four-fold aura, each aspect of which reflects the processes and qualities present in that body. These bodies manifest upon the various levels of consciousness or attenuated matter that form the personality or low-self, with the exception of course of the physical body which is made up of dense matter. There are other bodies on still higher levels, the buddhic and the atmic for example, and these also radiate auras, but it would take a highly superior form of clairvoyance to observe them. Despite the claims of some physics, I doubt it anyone with the capacity to see at those levels would discuss, much less write about what they could perceive. There is a point where the axiom 'he who knows, does not speak' begins to operate, so you may draw your own conclusions.

The chakras are an integral part of the subtle bodies of man. Various schools of thought list different numbers of them, and place them in different locations with respect to the physical body. The consensus once again, however, is that there are seven major chakras and these lie along the cerebro-spinal axis. The brow chakra lies upon the forehead, the crown chakra upon the vertex, the throat chakra near the first dorsal vertebra of the spine, the heart chakra between the shoulder blades. Beneath this stretches the diaphragm, symbol of the veil between the higher and lower worlds. Just below the diaphragm lies the solar plexus chakra, next the sacral chakra in proximity to the fifth lumbar vertebra, and finally the base chakra near to the coccyx.

These centres of force, or gateways of consciousness, are an important aspect of our study of the human aura, because they represent the seven levels of consciousness, and serve as points of entry to the inner worlds or heavens. At the physical and etheric levels they are bio-psychic resonators which activate our vitally important endocrine gland system, and maintain the health and integrity of our organ systems. As previously mentioned, the mystics and sages of old drew up maps of consciousness to guide us along the inner path to Self-realization, and the chakras are an integral part of this spiritual geography.

There are many meanings to the word chakra: a circular form, a potter's wheel, an astonomical circle. In *Layayoga* author Shyam Sundar Goswami writes:

A chakra is a circular form, having a specific centre.
It is situated within the body, not as a part of the gross body, but as a supra-material power form. It is imprinted undetectably in the body. Because of its subtle character a chakra is not seen by the eyes, even with the help of supersensitive instruments.

Goswami continues to write about the dense physical body, and to outline its relationship to pranic forces. His comment with regard to the chakras being beyond instrumented detection, in view of the work of Dr Hiroshi Motoyama, is interesting. Motoyama claims to have built a scanner that will pick up the chakras, but upon reading his material one cannot help feeling that in reality it detects the electrical fields of the nerve plexuses usually associated with each chakra rather than the vortice of energy itself.

Of the gross body and the primary energy of prana, Goswami has several vital points to make that are directly relevant to the point of view or interior posture we have to adopt in order to grasp the whole subject of these subtle worlds. Our focus of awareness is essentially physical, we are conditioned by current belief systems to think and be aware of the physical world. This form of perception is forced upon us in such a way that we forget that there are other ways of 'seeing' which are a natural function. The mechanistic belief that our mind arises from the chemical and physiological reactions in our physical brain is typical of science, but the sage and seer view the matter from an entirely different point. Goswami illustrates this quite clearly when he says:

> The material body is the effect of the metamorphosis of the basic energy which is made to operate on the surface stratum due to the influence of the prana-force. That basic energy is entirely matter-free and active in the substratum, but is endowed with a specific quality which, under certain conditions, gives it an inertial character. This basic energy exhibits a circular wave motion which is reducible to a subtle infinitesimal point.

The infinitesimal point in Tantric teaching is the bindu point. This point through concentration becomes a state of tremendous mental power, and is an indispensable part of the power expressed by the shaman or yogi in his practices. Through the bindu point in a chakra we can gain access to vast new areas of consciousness; they are literally points of power that lead the adept into other worlds, other universes. The Sufi shayks look upon the constellation of the Bear, as indeed the Gnostics appeared to, as seven cosmic chakras. Ruzbehan of Shiraz, an eleventh century mystic, penetrated into these points of power.

Then, I concentrated my attention on the constellation

of the Bear and I observed that it formed seven apertures through which God was showing himself to
me. . . .

Every night, I continued afterwards to observe
these apertures in Heaven, as my love and ardent desire
impelled me to do. And lo! one night, I saw that they
were open, and I saw the divine Being Manifesting to
me through these apertures. He said to me, 'I manifest to you through these openings; they form seven
thousand thresholds (corresponding to the seven prin-
cipal stars of the constellation) leading to the threshold
of the angelic pleroma. And behold I show myself to
you through all of them at once.'

To penetrate the bindu point is to enter a dimension of
awesome power, and it takes a great deal of preparation
and spiritual refinement. To enter unprepared, if indeed
that is at all possible, would in all probability prove fatal
to both physical and psychological health. Chakras are an
aspect of our subtle forms which need to be handled with
care. Pop occult literature which urges you towards
enlightenment and a better sex life through chakra stimulating exercises is a sort of pseudo-spiritual pornography,
which should be studiously avoided by the serious student.
The reason for this is simple: over-stimulation of any
chakra activates the pranic forces of that centre and begins
to open doorways to other areas of consciousness. The
problem is, once the stimulation has had effect, what
does the individual do with the energy he has contacted
and, more to the point, does he have the capacity and
perceptiveness to do anything with it? Chakras will unfold
in their own time and sequence, with of course the imbalances we bring about through our habits of thought,
emotions and physical living. To stimulate them hap-
hazardly through intense visualization and breathing
exercises may provide a weekend of fun at a workshop,
but if continued can lead to disaster. The participant may

find that the exercises have opened the faculty of clair-audience and that he is subjected to a non-stop babble of voices and communications in his head. He may experience a loud snap in his head, like a bone breaking. This is the rupturing of the etheric webs that protect and form insulation against unwarranted data flooding into consciousness from many different areas. When it breaks the result can be catastrophic to the individual, rendering him quite ineffective in daily life. A shift in energy from the sacral or sexual centre to the throat chakra may give him the illusion of a kundalini experience, which are all the rage at the moment. Such glamour only defers inner progress.

The bindu point has been known to the Vedic and Tantric adepts for many thousands of years. The bindu point and the chakra form a gateway, as Jung called it, to other levels of consciousness, other universes. It is a boundary point, which in time we will cross to a true understanding of the nature of reality. I am struck by the similarity between the bindu point of the ancient Vedic hymns and the singularity of modern science. I am convinced in fact that they are the same thing. In *God and the New Physics*, Paul Davies writes:

> The essential feature of a singularity is that it is rather like an edge or boundary to spacetime and hence, one supposes, to the physical universe.

and:

> In a fundmental sense a singularity represents, according to this view, the outer limits of the natural universe. At a singularity, matter may enter or leave the physical world, and influences may emanate therefrom that are totally beyond the power of physical science to predict, even in principle. A singularity is the nearest thing that science has found to a supernatural agent.

The similarities between a bindu point and the singularity are quite remarkable. It is thought that black holes in space form with a singularity, and that these huge vortices (chakras?) may lead to other universes on the exit side of the hole. The sages have always used the human body as a metaphor for the universe, ascribing various planets to various organs. If we are indeed a universe in miniature, then our chakras are the 'black holes' out of which the energies flow from the inner worlds to form our bodies. If this is so then the soul or transpersonal self is a type of bindu point, as must be the monad or spirit beyond that. The monad or One is often depicted as a point, and surely the journey of the prodigal son symbolizes for each of us the journey that will lead us through the bindu points of the chakras to those of the soul and ultimately the monad or Father's House. It is beyond our comprehension at that point to conceive of our form nature, if any, or the worlds we will enter to carry on the task allotted to man. An unknown saint of the Christian Church is recorded as having said: 'As birds fly together to summer realms, so souls unite in flight. Passing through the gate [bindu point] they thus alight before the throne of God.'

The chakras, as already mentioned, are described as a circular vortex form of energy. Each of them is depicted in a variety of ways, using deities, colours, symbols and letters to represent various qualities and energies. The most common form of expression is the use of a flower, which is appropriate in that the chakras should unfold naturally like flowers. The Rosicrucians used the Rosy Cross to depict man and his chakras; each rose on the cross identified a chakra in the subtle body. In India the lotus has been used as a symbol of the chakras, and they are often referred to as lotuses. The lotus is a flower that has its roots in the mud (the material world), its stem grows up through the water (the astral or emotional world), and the bloom rising above the water into the air (the realm of the mind) provides an excellent metaphor for the chakra.

The chakras are 'seen' through a deep form of clairvoyance arising out of concentration. The most popular map of the chakras, which is frequently adopted by authors who have perhaps not researched this area as much as they might have done, is that outlined by the theosophist C.W. Leadbeater. His monograph on the chakras has a number of fundamental inaccuracies in it which should perhaps be identified. The Bishop C.W. Leadbeater, for all of his fine work, was an astral psychic, and as such worked with certain involutionary energies when viewing things on the inner levels. For this reason he places the chakras along the front of the body, instead of along the cerebro-spinal axis. He also, for reasons of his own, removes the sacral chakra and replaces it with the spleen chakra. The seven major chakras, of which the spleen is not one, deal with various aspects and levels of consciousness. The spleen chakra does not. Its function is to energize the etheric body by way of the nadis; in other words it handles solar prana. Why he made the switch I do not know, but it is a gross error which has been promulgated ever since by non-psychics and psychics alike. Sir John Woodruffe, in his monumental work on kundalini, *The Serpent Power*, states quite openly that Leadbeater was of the opinion that he knew more about the chakras and kundalini than the yogis of India, and as a result inserted a few of his own ideas, despite the fact that they contradicted the models put forward by seers.

It will help us then to properly locate the chakras, beginning at the base of the spine and working upwards to the forehead. At the base of the spine, at the level of the coccygeal segments, lies the base or *muladhara* chakra. It has four petals, the colours of which vary according to different schools of thought. They are: a shining red and gold, yellow or golden, or red like the jawa flower. This chakra externalizes as the adrenal glands and governs the spine and kidneys. It also influences all cells of the body and is closely associated with the chrommafine tissue to be found in the adrenals, along the para-sympathetic nerve chains and in fact in every cell in our body. These provide the channel through which the physical will-to-be expresses itself, our fight or flight mechanism being the most obvious aspect of this force.

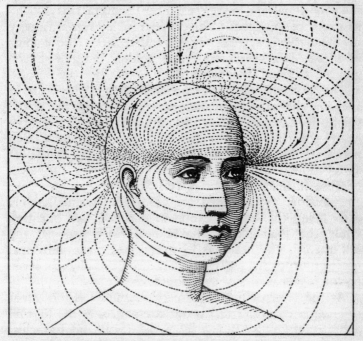

Figure 3.2 The psycho-magnetic curving lines of force which, according to Dr Edwin Babbitt, surround the human head. These lines of force can be mentally projected towards other people in order to tap their aura and make them turn around

Above the base chakra lies the sacral or *swadhisthana* chakra at the midpoint of the sacrum or sacred bone. This chakra externalizes as the gonads and governs the reproductive system. It has six petals of vermilion-red and diamond-white. Through this chakra flows the sexual energies that guarantee the continuation of the human race in physical form.

Next is the solar plexus or *manipura* chakra just around the level of the navel. It externalizes as the pancreas and governs the stomach, liver, gall bladder, digestive tract and the sympathetic nervous system. Here is the seat of the emotional and instinctual life. Its overactivity today in many people leads to digestive trouble, over-sensitivity of the nervous system, fatigue and tension. The colours of black, dark blue, dark green, golden, red and smoke-grey are ascribed to its ten petals.

The first chakra above the diaphragm is the heart or *anahata* chakra, located behind the heart in the dorsal spine. It externalizes as the thymus and governs the heart, the circulatory system and the blood. Its sixteen petals are said to be deep red, vermilion, white, dark blue and yellow. This is a most important vortex of power because ultimately when in full flower it expresses love and wisdom as expressed for us by Christ and Buddha, each being the leading exponent of those two qualities. While the solar plexus chakra deals with personal and self-interest, the heart, as it opens, makes the individual more group conscious, not so much on the physical level, but on higher planes of consciousness.

At the level of the lower cervical spine lies the throat or *visudda* chakra. This chakra externalizes as the thyroid and para-thyroids, and governs the vocal and bronchial apparatus, the lungs and digestive tract. The ancients saw the throat centre as the vortex through which the intelligence of God worked. It has sixteen petals — white, yellow and red going to a shining smokey-colour.

Next in order of importance is the brow or *ajna* chakra, which is located over the forehead. It externalizes as the pituitary gland and governs the eyes, ears, teeth, sinuses and lower brain, including the stem. This is the centre of the personality or low-self. When active in a balanced way you get the type of individual who sparkles with energy;

such females are vivacious, while males have the charisma that makes them popular with others. If too active it indicates the over-striver, the perfectionist who will sooner or later reach a state of nervous debility or breakdown due to the excess of energy flowing through this centre. Underactivity brings about a state in which the individual represses the energies of the personality, inclines to introversion and fails to fully express himself. The brow chakra has two main petals leading from a central circular area, which symbolize the anterior and posterior pituitary bodies, and ultimately the horizontal arms of the cross of matter upon which the personality is finally crucified. These petals are an intense white, like the moon, a symbol of the low-self. The ajna is considered by some schools to be the seat of mind, which has the power to reach anywhere into the source of all knowledge. Through this chakra the gift of higher mental clairvoyance is utilised.

Finally on the vertex of the head lies the crown or *sahasra* chakra. It externalizes as the pineal gland and governs the brain along with the rest of the central nervous system. It traditionally has a thousand petals the colours of white, red and yellow, black and green. This is the point of ultimate power, the Godhead in man. This chakra and the heart chakra are the last to unfold if a proper sequence has been followed. This unfoldment represents the balanced function of the will and the love and the wisdom of God. The esoteric meaning of the name David is 'he who has linked his head and his heart'. Daud in Celtic means 'beloved of God', and the Psalmist David who took thirty-three years to reach this point of initiation provides us with an insight into the healing power and wisdom that can be expressed through the uninterrupted interplay between the head and the heart chakras.

In the writings of the Tibetan Master Djwal Khul, there are two passages which reflect this quality: 'When the heart is full of love and the head full of wisdom, nothing then is ever done that can cause distress to others in the long run.' And: 'Joy settles as a bird within the heart but has winged its way from the secret place within the head. I am that bird of joy. Therefore with joy I serve.' A further passage indicates the qualities of energy and the links that exist between the crown, heart and throat chakras, which symbolize the three primary aspects of Deity: will, love-wisdom and active intelligence; or, if you prefer, Father, Son and Holy Spirit.

> Out of the lotus in the head springs the flower of bliss.
> Its earliest form is joy.
> Out of the lotus in the heart springs the flower of
> love. Its earliest indication, wisdom is.
> Out of the lotus in the throat emerges the flower of
> living forms. The earliest sign is understanding of
> The Plan.

The Plan of course refers to the grand design and intent of God, and not the short- or long-term plans of the personal self. Our chakras reflect our consciousness and according to their unfoldment so will be the quality of the auric field of the individual.

Various authors list varying colours for the chakras, for example red for the base chakra or green for the heart. The next thing you know someone else has listed orange and gold. Even the ancient schools of thought differed in the colours that they ascribed to the centres. There is good reason for this, and it lies in the fact that as the adept penetrates deeper and deeper into the chakra he 'sees' different colours. The Indian seers claimed that deep concentration on a chakra, particularly its colour-form, resulted in a resonance being set up with unknown regions of consciousness, which would eventually emerge as colours to the inner sight of the yogi. The colours change from one to another as specific pranas are activated in the chakra. This explanation is not confined to the Buddhist and Tantric systems but can be found among the Sufi mystics and their writings.

The Sufis call the chakras *Latifa*, the subtle organs of the mystical physiology. As you progress through the latifa you in effect progress through the seven prophets of your being. Of this process Corbin writes:

> The mystic is aware of this growth thanks to the apperception of coloured lights which characterize each of the supersensory organs or centers to which Semnani gave so much attention. These lights are the tenuous veils enveloping each of the latifa; their colouring reveals to the mystic which stage of his growth or journey he has reached.

Corbin goes on to list the colours. You will see just how closely they relate to those listed in Tantric texts, which suggests that the chakras are not just the figment of wild imagination, as some writers have more recently suggested.

> The stage of the subtle body at the level of its birth, still very close to the physical organism (the 'Adam of your being'), is simply darkness, a blackness sometimes turning to smoke-grey; the stage of the vital soul (Noah) is blue colour; that of the heart (Abraham) is red; that of the superconscious (Moses) is white; that of the Spirit (David) is yellow; that of the arcanum (Jesus) is luminous black (aswad nurani); this is the 'black light,' the luminous Night about which were informed by Najm Rāzī as well as by the Rose Garden of Mystery and its commentator; lastly the stage of the divine center (Mohammad) is brilliant green.

Obviously one must keep an open mind about the colours representing each chakra, because they can differ according to various schools of thought, they differ according to the viewing point of the adept and they differ again when discussed in relation to other factors in the physiology of light.

While I have concentrated on the Tantric and Sufi

explanations of the chakras, these force centres are mentioned in virtually all teachings. There are Taoist maps of consciousness that identify the chakras, and you can find them in the mystical alchelmical teachings of such Christians as Boehme and his disciple Gicthel. The former wrote: 'Now this wheel hath seven wheels one in another, and one nave, which fitteth itself to all seven wheels, and all seven wheels turn on that one nave.' Such a description tallies with the Tantric physiology of light, with the seven wheels or chakras upon the nave or vertical cerebro-spinal axis. Tribal societies seem less inclined to make public knowledge of these chakras, but the Aborigine of Australia sees all creation as arising from the great mystical vortex or Turinga, and they speak of the third eye on the forehead in conjunction with the *rai* spirits which give the shaman his inner sight.

The chakras, supersensory organs of light, the subtle bodies and the aura are aspects of man which are to be found in the teachings of all civilizations and societies throughout the world. For this reason alone they should provide a fruitful area of research today.

4

Science and medicine look at the aura

There cannot be the least doubt of the reality of the existence of an aura enveloping a human being, and this in a short time will be an universally accepted fact.

The Human Aura — Dr Walter Kilner

Man it seems cannot resist attempting to render the invisible visible to normal sight, by a mechanical apparatus of one type or another. In times gone by the aspirant to the Mysteries would discipline himself in order to develop clairvoyance, but we seem less inclined to make the requisite effort and take on the arduous training towards such ends. Being able to see the aura, particularly in the medical field, obviously has great advantages if you are able to interpret what you see in diagnostic terms. Dr Walter Kilner was a man determined to explore this field to the limits of his ability. Unfortunately this did not include clairvoyance so he was forced to discover an artificial means by which to make the aura visible. In 1908, whilst practising as a physician at St Thomas' Hospital in London, Kilner discovered and developed a process for making the human aura visible to those without the supersensory faculty of clairvoyance. He was well aware of Reichenbach's work with the odic force and sensitives, but Kilner wanted to see the aura for himself, and this forced him to seek a more physical approach which would be useful to others. In his book which was originally published under the title *The Human Atmosphere*, Kilner wrote:

> From the first moment of seeing the human atmosphere, I determined to investigate the subject apart from all occultism; and to remain unbiased, did not read any accounts of the aura until a large number of patients had been inspected.

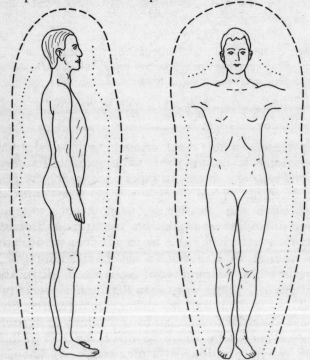

Figure 4.1 The outline of a healthy male aura according to Kilner

It was in the same year, 1908, that he came up with the idea of using some form of chemical to make the aura visible, and he began working with a coal tar dye called dicyanin. This choice of substance arose from a flash of inspiration triggered by his study of Professor Blondot's work on N-Rays at Nancy University in France, and in particular the effect N-Rays had upon phospherent sulphide of calcium. Kilner began by coating glass screen with gelatin and staining this coating with the dye. These proved to be quite useless due to the rapid decomposition of the gelatin. Eventually he settled on flat glass containers filled with an alcohol solution of the dye. Even these deteriorated if left in the light for any length of time, and had to be stored in darkness when not in use.

For general observations of the aura, Kilner used a dark screen in which the dye was less diluted, and a light screen which contained more alcohol. On completing the first screen Kilner was able to observe the aura of a friend through it. One can imagine his excitement as the greyish mist of the aura became apparent to his gaze. By experimenting Kilner found that by gazing through a dark screen at a light, and then looking directly at the person under observation, it was possible to see the aura without the screen. However, by far the most practical approach was to look at the subject directly through a light screen.

Having discovered a way to see the aura, Kilner not unnaturally spent every spare moment of his time gazing through the screens and noting his observations of the auric fields, which he began to plot. It was not long before he discovered that the screens had a deleterious effect upon his eyes, making them so painful and irritated that he would have to cease using them for several days at a time, allowing his eyes to return to normal. Kilner found that the aura was best observed when the light was not too bright, and the body of the subject just visible in the dimness against a dead black background.

According to his observations, Kilner divided the aura into three layers which he called the inner aura, the outer

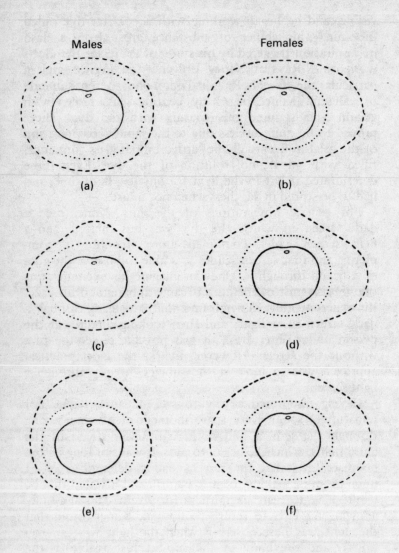

Males   Females

(a)   (b)

(c)   (d)

(e)   (f)

Figure 4.2 Transverse sections of male and female auras according to Kilner (a) and (b) normal auras; (c) and (d) spatulate auras; (e) and (f) auras with dorsal bow-shaped bulge

aura, and the ultra-outer aura. To these he added a fourth layer which he called the etheric double. This extended no more than one sixteenth to one eighth of an inch from the physical body, although in some pathological states it did appear to expand, particularly in neurotic patients. Kilner, it seemed, was not going to be able to ignore the occult, as he called it, and was soon using theosophical terminology, and confirming the descriptions of the etheric body given by clairvoyants. He writes:

> When the etheric double is examined against a white background through a deep carmine screen with the light properly arranged, it may become a rose colour, quite different to the carmine tint the white background has assumed. When carefully looked at this will appear lineated, and a fine striae [sic] to be the source of the colour.

The inner aura lies outside and around the etheric double. Kilner described it as having a finer texture to it. This was best observed through special screens containing carmine or methylene blue dye. With these the inner aura could be seen quite clearly and its outer border defined. In the process of his experiments Kilner developed a system for observing the aura with a series of screens, in order to make its various layers visible. He began his viewing with a general scan through the dicyanin screen, then switched to a pale blue one in order to see the differentiation between the inner and outer auras. The blue screen enabled him to map out the distal margins of the inner and outer auras but tended to obscure details of the former. Then, in order to heighten and clarify the appearance of the inner aura, he used another screen of light carmine dye. This tended somewhat to blur out details of the outer aura, but with various arrangements of lighting, a balance could be reached in which details from both auras were more or less visible. Kilner described what he could see through the screens in the following words:

In health the boundaries of the inner aura are determined by the distance the striae reach, when examined through the dark carmine screen. As a rule the breadth is uniform all over the head and trunk, and generally, but not always, slightly narrower down the limbs. Occasionally both in males and females it will become wider and coarser locally, but as striation can be discerned though perhaps with difficulty, there can be no uncertainty about limits. This is quite different to what takes place in local bodily derangements. The commonest position for enlargement is at the sides of the waist in women, and the next is the small of the back in a man, but a granular appearance in this latter situation is generally pathological, and will be described later on. Females show enlargements of the aura in front of the breasts and abdomen, and these will be alluded to in the chapter on pregnancy.

As a rule the inner aura follows the contour of the body, its proximal border being in juxtaposition to the etheric double, or in the majority of cases apparently to the body itself. The outer margin is free, irregularly crenated with large curves. The structure consists of excessively fine grains, so arranged as to present a striated appearance. The striae, too, are fine beyond description, parallel to each other, and running at right angles to the body. They show no intrinsic colour. They seem to be collected into bundles, with the longest lines in the centre, and the shortest outside. These bundles are massed together, and their shapes cause the outlines of the inner aura. In most people during health, striation is manifest, without the slightest difficulty, while in others of a delicate constitution or ill health, it can only be detected, if at all, by the most careful arrangement of the light, and the selection of a suitable screen.

Kilner's description of the inner aura is remarkably similar to those obtained through clairvoyant observation.

The lines of energy at right angles to the body, the coarse granulations which appear in ill health, all tally. Phoebe Payne, the theosophical clairvoyant who did such excellent work in the medical field with her husband, Dr Laurence Bendit, once likened the aura in health to a well strung tennis racquet, and an unhealthy aura looking for all the world like an unstrung one. Kilner goes on to describe the outer aura:

> The outer aura commences where the inner leaves off, and spreads round the body to a variable distance.
> It has no absolutely sharp outline but gradually vanishes into space, although in the majority of instances its outer border is sufficiently obvious for measurement.

Beyond this outer aura Kilner could distinguish, at times, a fine mist which extended outwards until it disappeared. This phenomenon he termed the ultra-outer aura. During observations, spontaneous fluctuations appeared throughout the aura in the form of rays. Some of these proceeded from one part of the body to another, while others streamed outwards and disappeared into space. Frequently, glowing patches appeared and faded out again. The rays were usually bluish in colour but some were red and yellow. Such rays, when emanating from the area of the shoulders, appeared broad, while those from the fingers were narrow and appeared to be continuous with the physical form. Some of Kilner's subjects could voluntarily change the colours in their auras through mental concentration. Women of an excitable nature showed the greatest facility for this gift.

Kilner experimented with various forces upon the aura, and found that if he held a magnet near the body, the aura became more brilliant in that area, and as the force grew the brilliance gathered into a single ray of light. If the magnet was moved the ray moved with it. Kilner noted that the mutual attraction of two human auras was far greater than that between an aura and a magnet. This is a point we should bear in mind, and one which I will deal with in detail in a later chapter. The use of static electricity to stimulate the aura provided Kilner with some interesting observations. Exposure to static electricity from a Wimshurst Machine caused the outer aura to contract within a fraction of a minute, and grow more dense, while at the same time the inner aura lost its distinctness. Then both auras lost their brilliance, and the inner one vanished altogether, while the outer aura contracted almost to the previous limit of the inner aura. Continued charging of the aura with static electricity caused the entire auric field to vanish. As this change began to dissipate, the auras began to reappear, and the after effect was an enlargement of the size of the aura, in some instances, by almost fifty per cent.

Kilner also applied various chemicals to the aura. Bromine vapour, for example, changed a previously blue-grey aura to a pure blue with areas of green. Iodine produced a red-brown colour in the aura as did ozone. He made various other experiments along these lines, and his observations suggest that medicines painted or rubbed onto the body alter the auric field and their therapeutic qualities are absorbed in this manner.

As a medical doctor Kilner was eager to explore the diagnostic potential of his methods of auric observation, which in themselves were quite unique. He found that the aura in pathological cases changed in shape and size, and in cases of nervous diseases, epilepsy, hysteria and hemiplegia it stayed distorted. If the disease process was a transient one, as it would be during infections or injury, then the aura returned to normal as the infection cleared or the injury healed. Impairment of mental faculties clearly created a lessening of the size and distinctness of the aura. A similar appearance occurred in people who were about to faint. Kilner was also able to observe that patients with limited intelligence had auras that were coarse-grained, grey and dull. In part this led him to believe that the aura had an intimate connection with the central nervous system.

Whilst doing remarkable work, Kilner still recognized that his methods of observation left much to be desired. His feelings about this are reflected in the following passage from his book:

> The alteration in the aura occasionally does not seem nearly commensurate with the severity of the illness, as many of the modifications are far too subtle to be detected by the crude methods of observation at the present time available, but it must be postulated that future and more delicate processes of investigation will disclose a greater number and variety of defects. The changes most likely to be discovered at the present time are differences in size and shape of the aura accompanied by alterations of the colour and texture.

Despite his limitations Kilner made many useful observations which will perhaps one day form the basis of fresh research. He established that the aura of a healthy person presented a symmetrical appearance through the screens, while a spatulate aura was most commonly seen in adult women of an hysterical nature. Traumatic hysteria revealed a bulging spatulate aura with large areas of yellow over the legs, chest and back. The epileptic aura on the other hand generally appeared narrow on one side, with an outer aura that was not much larger than the restricted inner aura. One of Kilner's patients, a woman with Raynaud's disease, displayed large areas of granulated redness around the chest, neck and back.

When comparisons are made between Kilner's work and clairvoyant descriptions of the aura, there are many similarities. But it is clear that although his method was revolutionary it did not provide such a detailed picture as could be derived from clairvoyant observation. He was well aware of these limitations but was convinced that physical methods would evolve until they became an aid to medical diagnosis.

It is a matter of record that many people who have tried to observe the aura with Kilner screens do not succeed in doing so. This led in time to the suggestion that Kilner himself was closer to being clairvoyant than he realized. Quite naturally his researches attracted the obligatory torrent of abuse from medical colleagues, and the *British Medical Journal* added its scorn, dismissing his work in the January issue of 1912, by writing: 'Dr. Kilner has failed to convince us that his aura is more real than Macbeth's visionary dagger.' Kilner did not let this scepticism deter him from his work and continued to experiment with the screens and record his observations.

The First World War put a stop to the experiments, as supplies of dicyanin from Germany were cut off. Kilner retired from practice and returned to Bury St. Edmunds to assist his brother in practice there. He died on 23 June 1920 at the age of 73. In that year a completely revised edition of his book had gone to press, and this was sympathetically and enthusiastically reviewed in the *Medical Times*, February 1921, and in March 1922 by the usually cautious *Scientific American*.

Kilner's work set other people along the path of aura exploration. One of these was Cambridge biologist, Oscar Bagnall. His book entitled *The Origin and Properties of the Human Aura* was published in 1937, and outlines Bagnall's efforts to duplicate and if possible extend Kilner's work. In the initial stages of his work Bagnall used the dicyanin screen, but soon sought a better alternative which he found in a more stable form of coal tar dye called pinacyanol. This was made into screens, and, being cheaper, was available to a greater number of investigators.

Bagnall's findings were very similar to Kilner's, in that he saw an inner and an outer aura. The inner aura, he wrote, varied in brightness with health and extended around the body by some three inches, but was discernible for a further distance of eight inches, beyond which he refers to it as an outer haze. This haze he described as being pale blue to pale grey in colour. Bagnall did not see the red, yellows, golds or browns that Kilner reported, and this led him to comment:

> I feel, however, that few of us can hope to see what Kilner saw, for he was undoubtedly singularly gifted in this respect — clairvoyant. I have tested most of his claims and I can vouch for the majority of them from my personal experience. Others I do not for one moment presume to doubt, though I have never been able to confirm them, because my eyes can see no further beyond the violet than most people's except of course artificially.

Bagnall found that a screen containing a solution of blue pinacyanol made the distal margin of the outer haze more obvious, and made the inner aura brighter and more clearly defined. Like Kilner he was to observe the rays of light extending from the outer edge of the inner aura, through the outer haze and into the environment. This as we shall see is an observation common to most descriptions of the aura by various investigators. Bagnall's work served to confirm Kilner's original experiments, but his main contribution was the improved pinacyanol screens for viewing.

In more recent years one or two medical doctors and health care professionals have made public their ability to see the aura, while others have been inclined not to reveal their abilities. Some have reported being able to know at a glance what was wrong with the patient, but to satisfy clinical and practice protocol they have run lab tests and made physical examinations in order to make it appear they reached their conclusions in the standard manner. Dr John C. Pierrakos, scientist and psychiatrist, has studied the energy fields of animals, crystals, plants and human beings clairvoyantly for a number of years, and has endeavoured to apply these observations in his practice located in New York.

Pierrakos describes what he refers to as a field phenomenon, which is related to body metabolism, with its
production of heat, activity, breathing rates and emotional
states. This field is also affected by humidity, ionization of
the air and atmospheric conditions. We float and swim in
this sea of energies filled with shimmering pulsating colours,
which constantly change. Pierrakos gives a somewhat
complex and more poetic description of the human aura
which is best described in his own words.

> When a person stands against a homogeneous back-
> ground, either very light (sky blue) or very dark (mid-
> night blue), and with certain arrangements so that
> there is a softness and uniformity in the light, one can
> clearly see, with the aid of colored filters (cobalt blue)
> or with the unaided eye, a most thrilling phenomenon.
> From the periphery of the body arises a cloudlike, blue-
> gray envelope which extends for 2 to 4 feet where it
> loses its distinctness and merges with the surrounding
> atmosphere. This envelope is brilliant and illuminates
> the periphery of the body in the same way as the rays
> of the rising sun light up the fringes of dark mountains.
> It swells slowly for 1 to 2 seconds, away from the body
> until it forms a nearly perfect oval shape with fringed
> edges. It remains in full development for approximately
> 1/4 of a second and then, abruptly, it disappears com-
> pletely. It takes about 1/5 to 1/8 of a second to vanish.
> Then there is a pause of 1 to 3 seconds until it reappears
> again to repeat the process. This process is repeated 15
> to 25 times a minute in the average resting person.
> (Quoted in Regush, 1974)

Pierrakos describes the 'envelope' as being divided into
three layers. First a dark blue-black layer near the body
about one eighth of an inch wide. Then a blue-grey layer
of three to four inches in width, and a third or outer layer

which is sky-blue and approximately six to eight inches wide. The first layer Pierrakos describes as being more like a dark space around the body. The second or intermediate layer is made up of multiple shapes and forms, and is particularly bright around the head. There are wave-like movements in it and corpuscular movements which appear similar to the Brownian movements seen under high magnification. Then there are linear movements of yellow and white rays similar to those seen by Kilner, which travel to the edge of the aura and out into space. The intermediate layer has the appearance of a blue shimmering liquid of outstanding brilliance. Pierrakos's impression of the aura is that it springs from a longitudinal core of energy within the physical body, which radiates outwards, passing through the skin to activate and excite the surrounding atmosphere, and thus form the three layers of the aura. This observation, in essence, agrees with Kilner's belief that the aura was intimately connected with the central nervous system.

While Kilner and Bagnall used the screens, Pierrakos was able to employ his supersensible faculties to obtain information about the aura. Both techniques are of course valid, and the observations of each of these men tend to confirm the structure and variations in the activities of the field. None of them makes mention of the chakras, which suggests that they are seen in a different manner, and requiring a capacity to penetrate into more subtle realms of matter.

In the tradition of von Reichenbach, neuropsychiatrist Shafica Karagulla worked with sensitives who could see the aura, and she had the advantage that at least two of the most gifted could also see the chakras. This work is outlined in her book *Breakthrough to Creativity*. Karagulla, being a physician, was interested in the diagnostic applications of clairvoyance with respect to the aura, and using a fellowship from the Pratt Foundation she set up a long-range programme of aura diagnosis research.

Karagulla was fortunate in that three of the sensitives she worked with had excellent gifts of what she referred to as HSP, or Higher Sense Perception. One of these sensitives, Diane by name, was a housewife and also the president of a business corporation. She was extremely gifted, and more important perhaps, her observations were both reliable and consistent. Karagulla describes her ability in the following passages:

> In order to make clear the experiments in medical diagnosis which follow, I must explain in general what Diane 'sees.' She can see the physical organs of the body and any pathology or disturbance in function. She has not studied medicine or physiology and often her descriptions are those one would expect of a layman. These descriptions are accurate and clear and easily translate into medical terms. Medical diagnosis has proved that Diane is correct and accurate in what she sees.

Diane describes the etheric body which serves as the energy matrix for the physical form, seeing it as a web of light frequencies, penetrating the body like a sparkling web of light beams. She is adamant that any imbalances in the physical body always show up first in the etheric body before they move through into a state where they become clinically identifiable. Diane had the extra capacity to see the chakras, which is something that not all psychics have.

> Within this energy body or pattern of frequencies she observes eight major vortices of force and many smaller vortices. As she describes it, energy moves in and out of these vortices, which look like spiral cones. Seven of these major vortices are directly related to different glands in the body. She describes them as also being related to any pathology in the physical body in their general area. The spiral cones of energy that make up

these vortices may be fast or slow, rhythmical or jerky. She sometimes sees breaks in the energy pattern.

In this outline she includes the spleen chakra, and then adds the alta major chakra which is located at the back of the skull in the area of the medulla oblongata. This chakra governs the spine, and in time links with the brow and crown chakras to form a field of energy which gives rise to the nimbus or halo around the head. Observation of the functional integrity of the chakras reveals their connection and relationship to pathological states in the physical body. It is here that Karagulla widens the whole context of aura research, because by bringing the chakras to the attention of researchers in the scientific field, she is begining to fill in the details of the subtle anatomy of man that have been overlooked by previous investigators. It is a most vital and important step, particularly in our understanding of disease, and the inner levels where it originates. Karagulla describes what Diane sees when looking at the chakras:

> According to her description it [the base chakra] is made up of four smaller spiral cones of whirling energy with the sharp points of the cones fitting into a center point. If there is any disturbance in this central point or core, then she looks for some pathology in the area. Breaks or disturbances in the spiral cone have to do with some function of the physical body in that area. If any of these major vortices show a dullness or irregularity or 'leak' in this central point or core, she looks for some serious pathology in the physical body in the area.

Diane was able to describe all of the textural details of the etheric body, as bright or dull, fine or coarse, tightly or loosely woven. Some etheric bodies displayed gaps and holes, others fragmented areas and textures that looked like scar tissue. She worked in various clinics with Karagulla, where they would sit at the back of the waiting room while Karagulla would pick out patients at random and have Diane describe what she saw with her inner sight. Subsequent perusal of the medical records of each randomly selected patient showed without any doubt that Diane could identify and describe pathological states with great accuracy. It is worth citing an example of her clairvoyance under these conditions where neither she nor Karagulla knew what was wrong with the patient until the records were pulled from the file, following her reading of the aura and chakras.

> A few days later we selected another patient at random in the waiting room at the Endocrine Clinic. The patient I discovered later had Graves' disease. Diane described the energy vortex at the throat as being too active. She saw red color in this vortex along with a dull gray color. All this meant poor and erratic function of the thyroid as far as Diane was concerned. She also described an erratic rhythm in the energy flow.
>
> When she looked at the thyroid itself she saw it as spongy and soft in texture. It did not look normal or healthy and was larger than it should be. The right side was not functioning as well as the left. The parathyroids appeared normal. Diane said that the patient had a tendency to become dizzy and had periods of great exhaustion.
>
> The medical diagnosis showed Graves' disease with an enlarged thyroid, the right lobe being larger. The patient suffered from rapid pulse, weakness, exhaustion and nervous tremors.

What had taken medical science weeks of laboratory testing and physical examination to determine, Diane had 'seen' and described in a few moments. Clearly there are advantages to being clairvoyant and being able to interpret what is 'seen' with such accuracy. Imagine the progress medicine would make if many physicians had such gifts, and the opportunity to utilize them for the benefit of their patients.

More recently, in the early 1970s, Los Angeles physician Brugh Joy went through a sudden and far-reaching transformation, which led him from the comfortable world of the orthodox practitioner into wider realms of healing work. A Phi Beta Kappa graduate of the University of Southern California and the University of Southern California School of Medicine, he interned at Johns Hopkins Hospital, was resident in internal medicine at the Mayo Clinic, a staff member of the Good Samaritan Medical Center in Los Angeles, and Assistant Clinical Professor of Medicine at the University of Southern California. In every respect this constituted a highly respectable medical background. The sudden illumination which transformed him also instantly healed him of a potentially terminal disease, and led to his rapid departure from a very promising professional career in medicine.

In his book *Joy's Way*, Joy describes what he calls dialogues with the Inner Teacher. From the dialogues have come a number of unique discoveries. One of them was the concept and processes of a self-healing technique which he called Command Therapy. This involved the principle of mental imagery and visualization for the purpose of combating disease. The technique has subsequently been taken up by hundreds of medical doctors and health care professionals, not least of these Dr Carl and Stephanie Simonton, who have applied it in the field of cancer treatment. Today, just over a decade later, the technique is used throughout the world by many thousands of people who seek to bring about self-healing.

Joy was also soon involved in trying to scan the energy fields of the body, and he describes how this came about:

My discovery of energy fields radiating from the body surface, like my discovery of the principles of Command Therapy, occurred in 1973 — and quite by accident. Since Eunice's death, late in 1972, my only teacher was the Inner Teacher, with whom I was in daily contact in morning meditation.

One day in my office I was examining a healthy male in his early twenties. He was lying quietly on the examining table. I finished listening to his heart and lungs and was approaching the examination of the abdomen. As I was feeling for the edge of the liver, just under the right lower rib cage, I felt a strange impulse to see whether I could detect energy radiating from the liver. It is a large organ and metabolically very active, with high internal temperatures.

Moving his hand at a distance from the body Brugh Joy found that the liver did not give off any detectable energy, but as his hand went over the solar plexus area it connected with what felt like a 'warm cloud' — further investigation showed that the cloud radiated three to four feet from the body and was cylindrical in shape. Astonished and mystified, he determined to bring this matter up with the Inner Teacher the next morning. The reply to his enquiry was simply to look further: 'There are other areas of the body that radiate similar fields. Map them.' For several months he followed this injunction and mapped out a whole series of these tube-like energy structures, having no idea what they were or what their function was, if any. Then one day, browsing in a Los Angeles bookshop he happened to take a book on Tantra Yoga from the shelf and open it to an ancient drawing that depicted these circular energy structures in much the same positions as he had located them through hand scanning. His astonishment was so great that he broke the calm silence of the bookshop, exclaiming out loud, 'My God! I have discovered the chakras.'

This discovery led to extensive work and investigation, and later Brugh Joy attempted in the hallowed halls of the British Museum to scan mummies to see if they still gave off such energy fields. Fortunately the British are used to all manner of eccentrics, but when Brugh opened his eyes after concentrating on the hand scanning of one mummy, he found that he had an amused audience of at least twenty-five people. While his conclusions about the quality and nature of the energy fields of mummies had to wait, he was quite clear as to the importance of the human life-field.

> I believe the energy fields reflect and influence the structure of the body and its organization into organ systems. I also suspect that the chakra system is a mechanism that interrelates the gross physical body and the subtle or etheric bodies. I further believe that the chakra system, the physical body and the etheric body are in some sort of relationship with the meridians of the acupuncture system. The energy that emanates from the chakras and the energy that flows through the acupuncture meridian system are one and the same thing; the energy is either qualified by the chakra system or somehow refined by an individual chakra. I believe there is but one basic energy operating in these interrelated systems and that the chakra system modulates and transduces that basic energy. The body splays this one primary energy into its component frequencies just as a prism splays light.

Those words sum up for us most clearly the interrelatedness of these systems and the basic energy of prana. For anyone who wants to make a serious study of the techniques of hand scanning the aura, *Joy's Way* provides a great deal of information regarding techniques. His contribution to this field has a breadth and depth born of inner knowledge, thus his suggestions as to the practical applications of this work can be taken to heart by the sincere aspirant to healing.

There can be little doubt that orthodox science and medicine will have little or no time for the human aura, much less the chakras, until such time as someone devises an electronic scanner to replace the psychic. It was the same story with acupuncture. As far as orthodox medicine was concerned acupuncture was some form of Chinese medicine that made no sense, and certainly had no basis in fact. Meridians and acupuncture points, and talk of the life-force chi, were so much superstition and rubbish as far as science was concerned. Then a rather embarrassing event took place, viewed by millions of people in Britain. A group of British doctors were shown, during a trip to China, watching major surgery on the lung of a Chinese patient, while he was fully conscious. The only anaesthetic he had was a needle placed in his right forearm, and this was manipulated from time to time in order to maintain the effect. As the surgeons opened up the chest cavity, the patient smiled, chatted with onlookers, drank tea and ate biscuits. Astonished doctors later sprang a surprise visit on the patient following the surgery and found him sitting on his bed chatting with relatives and clearly in no way suffering from post-operative shock as may have been expected with orthodox methods. This scenario opened the door for acupuncture to become respectable. Orthodoxy is of course now busy trying to fit this embarrassing anomaly into a mechanistic framework — rigid attitudes die hard when it comes to dealing with vitalist concepts, and people who hold them will go to any lengths to find a 'respectable' scientific explanation for something that clearly lies outside of their narrow domain.

The advent of Kirlian photography caused quite a flurry of excitement in the 1970s when investigators in the field of parapsychology were of the opinion that this form of electro-photography had succeeded in capturing the human aura on film. Electro-photography had been around a long while, since the end of the last century in fact, but it took Ostrander and Schroeder's book, *Psychic Discoveries behind the Iron Curtain*, to popularize Kirlian photography and virtually make it a household name.

An enormous amount of work was done, some of it

carefully carried out, but a great deal of it rather haphazard. A lot of wild and extravagant claims were made. The process involves an arrangement of electrodes coupled to a high voltage source. To photograph the discharge of energy around a finger tip, a metal electrode with a dielectric plate above it is connected to a source of electricity. The film, emulsion side up, is placed on the dielectric, and the subject then places his or her finger tip on the film while an electrical voltage is punched through the plate. This whole procedure is carried out in darkness, so no light touches the film. The results are sometimes spectacularly beautiful, especially when the subject is highly charged with the life-force. The coronal discharge that appears on film is often an electric-blue, with areas of brilliant white and red, and investigators can be forgiven for claiming they had photographed the aura.

The Russians who spearheaded this work claimed that they could derive relevant information regarding the mental, emotional and physical states of a person from the intensity and quality of the flares that appeared on film. There is still a degree of controversy about this, and in some sectors of the scientific community this has been dismissed as highly unlikely. If the colours surrounding objects photographed in this manner are not auric, then what are they? In an article entitled 'Are psychoenergetic pictures possible?' in *New Scientist*, Professor William Tiller of Stanford University, California, writes:

> Is it rational to hope to observe a nonphysical manifestation directly, using only instruments fashioned after the five physical senses? I think not. We can only expect to detect information at the physical level. By nonphysical energies is meant energies of a nonelectromagnetic, nonsonic and nongravitational variety.

There is a scientific explanation for the beautiful coronal discharges that appear in Kirlian photographs, involving electrons and ionization and photons of light; so, alas, it appears that the aura has not been photographed after all, at least not according to science. Professor Tiller has said that the energy discharge seen on the film is physical in nature, taken with instruments geared to the five senses, but before we dismiss Kirlian photography we should remember that from an esoteric point of view the etheric body is physical, and does involve the atomic levels of matter in its make-up, so perhaps after all we are seeing the lowest aspect of the aura revealed by electro-photography. As I have mentioned earlier in the book, the important thing is that whatever the pictures reveal, whether it is the aura or not, they should serve to open the door and to inspire further studies along these lines.

In recent years another form of energy photography has emerged which may have some correlation to the aura. This technique is known as the Schlieren system. Originally it was developed to detect flaws in glass, but when used to photograph the convection currents created by heat given off by the human body, these appear as a shimmering, rainbow-coloured aura, according to David Heiserman of *Science Digest*. Scientists studying the heat convection currents of the body report that these currents are laden with microscopic bits of skin, bacteria and particles of inorganic matter. The heat envelope or halo contains four hundred per cent more micro-organisms than the immediate environment, and may in fact be in some way responsible for persistent infections that are difficult to clear from the body. The bacteria simply live and possibly breed in the heat aura, and move into the body when resistance drops. Observations of the warm air flow clearly reveal that it moves up the body and is drawn into the nose, thus probably enhancing the infective process.

Convection currents, like those seen shimmering over a desert landscape, can break up light into the colours of the spectrum in much the same way as a prism does. Because of this phenomenon the warm air envelope around the human body, when photographed by the Schlieren method, appears as a field of colour patterns. These colours change dramatically when there is heavy infection in the body, or areas of inflammation are present. Could it be that these colour patterns which change with disease are in some way connected with what psychics see? There are many similarities. For example the flow of convection currents as seen through the Schlieren optical system is virtually identical to the movements of the aura as described by Dr Pierrakos. He sees a basic flow pattern moving up from the feet to the head and back again, with alternate upward and downward movements of the aura on opposite sides of the body. Another interesting flow of the aura appears to form a figure eight over the body, with its central point in the area of the solar plexus. In chiropractic treatment, there is a method by which this 'eight flow' can be demonstrated. The patient is muscle tested, that is a muscle is tested by pressure from the doctor's hand, against his resistance. A strong muscle will remain firm — once a muscle tests strong it can be weakened by passing a hand close to the patient's back in a figure of eight movement. If the direction of the movement is right for the patient, the muscle will remain strong; if it is not, the muscle will immediately go weak. Having induced the weak reaction, this can be eliminated by moving the hand through the figure of eight in the right direction. The patient's body is not touched during this movement, which flows through the auric field. The fact that there is an immediate and physically demonstrable reaction in the neuro-muscular system of the patient brings further evidence to bear that Kilner was right when he surmised that the aura had a direct connection with the central nervous system.

The similarities between psychic and Schlieren descriptions of the aura, and the changes that take place in it due to disease processes, are marked. Whether the scientist and the psychic are seeing the same things is open to debate, but doctors working with the Schlieren system claim that they can diagnose from the patterns it makes visible. Gradually these similarities may well prove to be an open sesame, providing the much needed link between science and the esoteric teachings regarding the human aura.

One of the most substantial and outstanding contributions to our knowledge of man as an energy being made its appearance in 1935, when embryologist Dr Harold Saxton Burr and his colleague Dr F. Northrop published their work under the title 'The electro-dynamic theory of life'. In collaboration with Drs C. Lane and L. Nims, Burr spent three years perfecting an ultra-sensitive vacuum tube microvoltmeter which could measure currents as weak as a millionth of a volt between two points within or on a living organism. The voltmeter revealed that all living organisms have an electro-dynamic field which in effect acts like a 'jelly mould' of energy into which the physical form is built. To understand this better it helps to visualize a piece of paper with a scattering of iron filings over it. When a magnet is placed underneath and in proximity to the paper, the iron filings rush to form a pattern. In other words the electro-magnetic forces draw the inert iron filings into alignment along an axis, from which patterns of force splay out to give us a picture of the field. The sense of life that the magnet gives to the iron filings can be quite fascinating. Every life-form has such a field, and in our case this field guarantees more or less that with the renewal of new material to form our body, we will remain recognizable to our friends. If the electro-dynamic mould were to constantly change its shape our features would follow suit. Trauma to the physical body also traumatises the field; thus a scar will remain unless surgically removed, or the phantom leg will itch or irritate the amputee. Electro-magnetic fields then are the organizing 'mechanisms' that keep the physical life-form in shape and carry out maintenance and repair through the constant inflow of new material.

Burr and his colleagues spent well over thirty years carrying out painstaking experiments with the vacuum tube voltmeter. They found that voltage gradients rose and fell in trees that were monitored, and these perturbations fell into patterns that related not only to the seasons, but to phases of the moon and sunspot activity. Ovulation in women was directly related to a sharp rise of energy in the electro-magnetic field, which can be measured as a voltage-rise occurring in the middle of the menstrual cycle during a period of twenty-four hours. Changes in the life-field, or L-field as it was later called, could determine the presence of malignancy with a high rate of accuracy. A great deal of work was done along these lines by a Dr Langman of New York's Bellvue Hospital, using a voltmeter. With the aid of an assistant he examined one thousand female patients, placing electrodes on the cervix and ventral abdominal wall. Of these, 102 cases showed abnormal voltage-gradients, which suggested the presence of malignancy. Exploratory surgery confirmed that ninety-five of the 102 had cancer.

On 24 April 1948, Dr Leonard J. Ravitz, a star pupil of Burr's, demonstrated to the amazement of colleagues that subjects under hypnosis showed marked changes in their voltage-gradients. For the first time man had demonstrated a method of actually measuring the depth of hypnosis, and, more important, that the mind produces measurable effects upon the life-field. In his outstanding research Ravitz found that mentally instable people display varied and erratic patterns in the voltage potential of their L-fields, and that it would be possible to predict accurately the forthcoming reactions of seriously disturbed mental patients to magnetic storms in space. There are innumerable potential uses for the vacuum tube voltmeter which have yet to be thoroughly investigated. Burr's work, although of monumental importance, has had a very low key reception in scientific circles. This is perhaps due to the fact that during his lifetime Saxton Burr was a very low key person, who knew the wisdom of this posture. In any event his attitude has perhaps contributed to the absence of any real vilification of his work by his peer group. Better perhaps this way, in that later it can emerge as perhaps one of the most important discoveries of this century. The day will come, I am sure, when men of science will go back to Burr's work and use it as the basis upon which to build a whole new model of the physical and subtle anatomy of man.

The similarities between Burr's L-field and the formative etheric matrix of the Vedic teachings are total and unassailable. Too much so, in fact; one of the reasons why many scientists shied away from the electro-dynamic theory of life is because it had too many mystical implications for comfort. However, the similarities between the L-field of science and the etheric body of the ancient teachings run parallel to each other, and this is a fact that will bide its time until the more perceptive men of science admit the connection, and plan their research on that basis.

The evidence suggests that through the work of Kilner and Bagnall, and through the researches and experimentation of physicians like Karagulla, Brugh Joy and Saxton Burr, a body of material is gathering. If we add the visual displays of Kirlian and Schlieren photography with their similarities to clairvoyant explanations regarding the aura, then the body of material that is gathering will in the not too distant future become a critical mass, and we shall then be witness to a whole change of attitude. The word aura will move into everyday use, and people will say 'Well, why didn't I think of that?' and 'Yes, well, it was pretty obvious, wasn't it?' Thus a vital concept that has been held at bay by the barriers of the conditioned mind fills the vacuum of our ignorance and we move forward in our understanding to a more holistic picture of man and his inextricable relationship to all life-forms.

5

Colours of the auric field

Colour is, therefore, a Divine Force — nothing less!

The Seven Keys to Colour Healing — Roland Hunt

To clairvoyant sight the human aura is alive with glowing
ethereal emanations and coruscations of colour, far more
radiant and beautiful than those seen through the Kilner
screens, or captured on film by Kirlian or Schlieren photography. These flares and flickerings of colour reflect our
emotions and give form to our thoughts, their delicacy
and intensity express our spirituality and compassion, our
fears and prejudices. Colour, as we know, is a form of
vibratory energy. Its frequencies can be measured scienti-
fically in millimicrons, or mμ, ranging from red at 625-
750 mμ through to violet at 400-450 mμ. To the spiritual
sciences however, these colours have a far deeper meaning
and a whole symbology of their own. According to the
Mystery Teachings a vast hidden central sun irradiates
the whole of creation with seven creative energies known
as the rays; to each ray is designated one of the colours
of the spectrum and these form the seven primary qualities
which manifest in the temperaments of man, and govern
all life-forms from a planet to an ant.

When the Sufi sage, in deep meditation, penetrates the essence of the seven major stars of the constellation of the Bear, he sees seven apertures in the Throne of God, which are the gateways to the inner realms. The Christian mystic Jacob Boehme speaks of the seven rays as the Seven Fountain Spirits, and in the Bible they are referred to as the Seven Spirits before the Throne of God. From these flow the energies which activate our chakras and set up the flow of light and colour through our auras.

Each ray confers certain physical and psychological characteristics upon the individual, and determines his emotional and mental responses to life. Each predisposes us to certain weaknesses and gives us certain strengths. Our limitations, specific talents and capacities arise from the ray energies, and they govern how we handle our relationships with others. They colour, qualify and sound the note of our lives, and even mould our physical appearances. When we know which combination of the seven colour rays goes into our make-up, we can more readily gauge our capacities, opportunities and limitations, grasp the broad sweep of history, and learn how to relate in a warm and loving manner.

Alice Bailey wrote extensively on the rays, some five volumes in fact, so it is not a subject that reveals its secrets to cursory study. The basics however are simple and provide us with important material with respect to understanding the energies which flow throughout the aura. In *Esoteric Psychology*, vol. 1, Bailey writes:

Every individual vibrates to some particular measure. Those who know and who work clairvoyantly and clairaudiently find that all matter sounds, all matter pulsates, and all matter has its own colour. Each human being can therefore be made to give forth some specific sound; in making that sound he flashes forth into colour, and the combination of the two is indicative of some measure which is peculiarly his own.

And:

> The clue lies in the similarity of colour, which entails
> a resemblance in note and rhythm. When, therefore,
> a man is on the red and yellow rays, with red as his
> primary ray, and meets another human being who is
> on the blue and yellow rays, with a secondary resemb-
> lance to yellow, there may be recognition. But when a
> man on the yellow and blue rays, with yellow as his
> primary colour, meets a brother on the yellow and red
> rays, the recognition is immediate and mutual, for the
> primary colour is the same.

We have all, I am sure, had the experience of meeting a
total stranger with whom we feel an immediate rapport.
In esoteric circles it is fashionable to put this down to
having met in a previous incarnation, and while this may
be so, the fact is that the recognition most likely sprang
spontaneously from a similarity of ray patterns.

What then are the rays, their colours and characteristics?
Bailey lists the rays in the following manner, giving a
colour from the visible spectrum to each.

1st ray	Power, will and purpose	Red
2nd ray	Love-wisdom	Blue
3rd ray	Active, creative intelligence	Yellow
4th ray	Harmony through conflict	Orange
5th ray	Concrete science or knowledge	Green
6th ray	Idealism or devotion	Violet
7th ray	Order or ceremonial magic	Indigo

The above is a very useful and basic guide to the rays
and their colours, but once again we must not get confused
when we read, for example, that the rays have both
exoteric and esoteric colours. Having told us that the first
ray is red, Bailey lists the exoteric colour as orange and
the esoteric colour as red, which tallies; but then you look
at the third ray and find that, having said its colour is
yellow, she then throws us a curve by stating that the

exoteric colour is black and the esoteric, green. Again and again you will find apparently contradictory statements about colours and relationships of energies. The reason for this is two-fold: in the first place blinds are introduced into writings on esoteric matters in order to keep the neophyte from certain areas of knowledge — Blavatsky was apparently a dab hand at this form of expression; secondly, as we have already seen, colours alter with the depth of penetration into the area or energies under consideration. So the conflicting lists of colours do not in reality conflict at all. As a matter of interest I will include here the colours and jewels that theosophic writer Geoffrey Hodson attributes to the rays.

1st ray	White-fire, electric-blue, vermilion	Diamond
2nd ray	Golden yellow, azure blue	Sapphire
3rd ray	Emerald Green	Emerald
4th ray	Tawny bronze	Jasper
5th ray	Lemon yellow	Topaz
6th ray	Roseate-Fire	Ruby
7th ray	Purple	Amethyst

Every human being is essentially an expression of five ray forces. There are others, for example the ray of the Monad or Spirit, but this lies outside the purposes of our study. We have then:

The ray of the soul or transpersonal self
The ray of the mental body
The ray of the emotional body
The ray of the physical/etheric body
The ray of the personality

Let us return to the characteristics of the rays, for they are expressions of the colours flowing through the aura. Bailey and another writer, Michal Eastcott, outline these characteristics. While Bailey is perhaps more technical in her writings, Eastcott simplifies without losing any of the essence. Her books, 'I' The Story of the Self and

The Seven Rays of Energy, are excellent aids in the study of the ray qualities.

RED — 1st ray of Will and Purpose
Purposefulness
Natural leadership
Positivity and drive
Strength of will
Directness
Ability to initiate, lead and govern
Fearlessness

On a more negative level it can express itself as:

Ambition and arrogance
A love of power
Impatience and irritability
A domineering attitude
A conviction of being right
Tyranny
Pride
Contempt
Rigidity

Geoffrey Hodson states that this is the ray of the soldier, explorer, ruler, statesman and leader. The first ray man approaches life by sheer force of will. Napoleon was first and fourth ray, red and orange. Kitchener was first and seventh, the latter giving him a powerful ability to organize. Kitchener's colours, then, would be red and indigo.

BLUE — 2nd ray of Love-Wisdom
Understanding
Compassion
Patience
Persistence
Serenity
Faithfulness
Love of truth

Intuition
Serene temper
Clear intelligence

Some of the vices of this ray express themselves as:

Negativity
Over-sensitivity
Self-pity
Fear
Poor self-image
Introspection
Over absorption in study
Contempt of mental limitations in others
Indifference to others
Coldness

This is the ray of the healer and teacher, sage and reformer, working through co-operation and persuasiveness, usually with excellent tact and foresight.

YELLOW — 3rd ray of Creative, Active intelligence
Creative ideation
A clear intellect
Business acumen
Practical efficiency
Adaptability
Sincerity of purpose

The third ray may also confer the following characteristics:

Excessive activity and restlessness
A tendency to talk and move rapidly
Absent mindedness
Intellectual pride
Self-centredness
Deviousness

This is the ray of the philosopher, scholar, business man, strategist, banker and economist. He makes an excellent historian who will dig out and verify facts with great patience, when his third ray is complemented by the fifth.

ORANGE — 4th ray of Harmony through Conflict
Strong affections
Sympathy
Physical courage
Artistic creativity
Appreciation of the relationships between colour
Spontaneity and joy
Quickness of intellect

On the negative side the fourth ray can express itself as:

Ambivalence, vacillation and instability
Inaccuracy
Lack of moral courage
Impulsiveness
Moodiness
Self-centredness
Worry
Extravagance

This is the ray of the person of artistic temperament. Often the fourth ray person is torn by innner conflict as the higher and lower forces of their nature battle for supremacy. They may be wild speculators or gamblers when carried away by the fiery side (*rajas*) of their natures, or indolent and a moral coward when the tamasic (inertia) aspect of their nature dominates.

GREEN — 5th ray of Concrete Science or Knowledge
Careful analysis and examination
Discrimation
Justice without mercy
Perseverance
Common sense
Uprightness

Independence
Clear and concise mental concepts
Analytical and logical mentality

Some of the vices of the fifth ray are:

Narrowness
Harsh criticism
Unforgiving temper
Lack of sympathy
Prejudice
An intense materialism
Constant analysis
Divisiveness

The fifth ray person is usually impersonal and independent. You may have noticed this energy in expression when you last consulted a medical specialist on the National Health. They make excellent heads of technical departments, good engineers and chemists.

VIOLET — 6th ray of Idealism or Devotion
Altruism
Dedication
Single-mindedness
Love
Tenderness
Loyalty
Reverence

Its more negative aspects are very apparent in the world today, taking the form of:

Nationalism
Blind devotion
Narrowness and rigidity
Messianic convictions
Militant fanaticism
Strong emotions
Over-leaning and dependence upon others
Guru-worship carried to extremes

The person on this ray is full of religious impulses and intense likes and dislikes. They will burn you at the stake to save your soul, and march on crusades. They never make good statesmen or businessmen. At best they are saints, at worst a martyr or bigot.

INDIGO — 7th ray of Order or Ceremonial Magic
Strength
Perseverance
Extreme care in details
Self-reliance
Discipline
Orderliness
Great ability to plan and organize
Dignity, noble bearing

The vices of the seventh ray are:

Self-opinion over-indulged
Formalism
Pride
Bigotry
Narrowness

This is the ray of the priest-healer, the court official, the shaman who can invoke the elemental forces through ritual. It is the ray of form, ideal for the sculptor to have in his make-up. A person on this ray may be superstitious, with a deep interest in omens and dreams, occult practices and spiritualist beliefs. Often they are a great social success, saying the right thing at the right time.

As far as our study of the aura is concerned these rays are powerful streams of colour which bring qualities to life within our energy fields. Their characteristics will bring their appropriate colours into the aura, thus providing a guide to interpretation of what is seen — and correct interpretation is the nub of any aura reading.

From this model of the ray energies in nature, we can set up a construct of how they would appear in an individual. The layout in Figure 5.1 is one I devised for my own use in healing work. To this diagram we can add a set of ray energies, and then outline a brief interpretation.

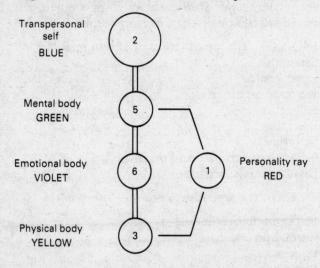

Figure 5.1 A model of the ray energies in an individual

The ray of the personality arises when the lower-self consisting of the mental, emotional and physical bodies are reasonably active and functioning in unison. Eventually the conflict between the ray of the soul and the ray of the personality reaches a pitch of intensity where it becomes known as the Arjuna experience. This battle and its attendant details are all clearly outlined for us in the *Bhagavad Gita*. From life to life the rays of each body tend to change, so that we gain experience in the balance and right control of all the forces that can enter into our make-up. However let us return to our hypothetical individual as illustrated by the chart.

This individual has blue and red as his primary colours. The blue (second) ray places him on the path of the teacher/healer. As we have read, it confers calmness, strength, patience and endurance, with a strong intuitive ability and clear intelligence. The negative side may express itself in coldness towards others, indifference and possibly contempt. Introversion, poor self-image, fear, negativity and anxiety are also part and parcel of this ray.

The green ray (fifth) of the mental body gives common sense, independence, a keen intellect, and quite often a belief in justice according to the letter of the law. It can give rise to a critical nature, arrogance, prejudice and a lack of sympathy. This kind of mind needs measurable proof of things, and is the ideal ray for the scientist, engineer, or researcher.

The violet ray (sixth) of the emotional body is devotional and idealistic by nature, loving and single-minded, with a strong sense of loyalty. On the negative side it can confer selfishness, partiality, prejudice and a fiery anger. It is the ray of fanaticism, narrow-mindedness and rigidity. There may be too much intensity of feeling and a reluctance to change.

The yellow ray (third) of the physical body will give sincerity of purpose, a capacity for concentration on philosophic subjects and a rather cautious nature characterized by patience. Equally it can bring absent mindedness, intellectual pride, obstinacy and a tendency to isolation. The yellow ray person tends to make much of being busy, and preoccupation with too many details can result in paralysis of action, and critical appraisals of others and their work.

The red ray (first) of the personality gives him strength, courage, the power to organize and direct. Along with this may come a measure of pride, arrogance and wilfulness, and certainly a desire to control others, a love of power and authority.

There are of course many other qualities and characteristics to these rays, and our subject would have some of them more dominant than others. This person would make a better teacher or instructor than he would a healer, because he carries a preponderance of the will aspect in his make-up as opposed to the love aspect. He has only the second and sixth rays to soften his nature. His fifth ray mental body might well lead him into science, engineering or possibly he may become a surgeon of high technical capacity. His sixth ray emotional body would give him a rather idealistic attitude, a narrow point of view and a tendency to be intolerant. These qualities would be magnified by his first ray personality and his third ray physical. The latter confers the ability to handle money and do well in business, and coupled to his fifth ray mind would most likely make him piercingly critical of others, and given to a fast manner of speech and physical action. In a classroom or work situation his first ray personality would almost certainly make him quite arrogant and dictatorial. He would come across as a loner, enjoying solitude. Certainly he is a person who would have to make a real effort to love others and show warmth and consideration. His aura would carry a sense of aloofness, not easily approached. He carries his own space with him rather like an encircling shield, which is hard enough to give a real sensitive a psychic bruising.

The colours seen in the aura are not necessarily those of the rays, because thoughts and emotions produce various flares and pulsations of colour in the aura. These may come and go in rapid sequence, or remain as a fairly constant pattern if there is a particular line of thought or emotion that is dwelt upon. Persistent obsessive thought patterns can create cleavages in the aura through which entities may find access, or elemental beings take possession. Physical and emotional trauma can scar the substance of the aura, leaving discolourations in the subtle matrix. The ray colours are of a deeper and more fundamental nature than the welter of other reflections in the aura, and can only be discerned by the highest form of inner sight. Having said this, in very practical terms they can be identified through plain common sense and observation of people's interests, actions and everyday behaviour.

Different authors and clairvoyants ascribe different meanings to the colours seen in the auric fields. Some agree with each other as to meaning, and quite naturally others do not. Obviously each clairvoyant who views the aura of another person does so through his own energy field, and for this reason he colours what he sees and this in turn influences his interpretation. However despite the differences there are many factors relative to auric colours about which most psychics agree. These make up a useful guide to those exploring this field, and who are learning to 'see' the aura for themselves. I will list some of these colours and their meanings to serve as a basis to build upon, but it must be kept in mind that certain colours will have certain meanings for you that may not be so useful to others. What follows is a broad consensus of opinion, a commonality of colour meanings.

RED

This is a predominantly physical colour, the symbol of life. It denotes strength, force, vigour, passion and capability. Light red in the aura may indicate a nervous, impulsive almost hyperactive person, whereas dark red can denote a fiery temper or sensuality. Red almost always means nervous trouble and over-concern about self. Pride, avarice and selfish affection show up as red; the last may have black intermixed with it. Individuals with a lot of red in their aura are often physically strong and wilful, with a rather materialistic outlook on life in general. Inflammatory states like arthritis show up as red in the auric field.

ORANGE

Bright orange indicates vitality and health. This colour when played upon the aura will help to step up the vital forces of the etheric body, thus imparting a sense of increased vitality. It often indicates a strong, vital personality, self-control, thoughtfulness, consideration, intellectual development, pride, ambition and selfish goals. Orange is often looked upon as a symbol of wholesomeness.

YELLOW

This colour indicates intellectual ability, well-being, friendliness and optimism. In some people the paler yellows can denote timidity, weakness of will-power and indecisiveness. Edgar Cayce said that people with yellow in their aura usually took good care of themselves, were happy, helpful and friendly, and not inclined to worry. Yellow is symbolic of clear mental processes, and a golden yellow can be an indication of developing spirituality. Yellow is a tonic for the nervous system, vitalizing not only the physical body but the mind and emotions too, imparting a sense of optimism.

GREEN

Green is the colour of nature and of healing, especially if allied to blue. It is beneficial to have a good clear green in the aura, but darker tones can be related to deceit, cunning and falsehood. A lemony-yellow is said to be a clear sign of deceitfulness. People with green in their auras are usually lively, thoughtful, versatile and adaptable. Green governs the mental levels of consciousness and indicates a plethora of ideas. It is the colour of regeneration, new life springing up, prosperity and success. Cayce says that doctors, nurses and health care professionals invariably have a lot of green in their auras. People can become green with envy, and when this is tinged with reddish-brown or murky red it denotes jealousy. Sympathy and adaptability, according to Leadbeater, show up as green in the aura.

BLUE

This is the colour of high-mindedness and great thoughts, according to Cayce. It denotes idealism, devotion, spiritual feelings, self-reliance and confidence. A bright blue in the aura shows loyalty, sincerity and integrity. Dark blue is associated with wisdom and saintliness. It is the symbol of prayer, contemplation and meditation. Pale blue may indicate superficial talents and is connected with the struggle to become established; as the blue deepens it denotes a flowering of ability. Blue is associated with moodiness, gloom and sadness. Black mottling on blue arises from selfish religious feelings, whereas aqua-blue reflects pure religious feeling.

VIOLET

This is the high spiritual colour of the adept and initiate. It indicates love, wisdom, soul power and true greatness. Some psychics claim that this colour is seldom seen in the aura of the average person.

INDIGO

This colour in the aura is an indication of high spirituality and persistence in seeking after deep spiritual truths. It can indicate a change in relationships and may in some instances represent internal poisons. Indigo is the colour of synthesis and psychic faculties, benevolence, coolness and calmness.

BLACK

Black indicates malice and hatred, and when linked to anger appears as coils of heavy poisonous looking smoke in the aura, according to Leadbeater. It is associated with bad deeds, discord and evil thoughts. Ouseley says that in the most devilish and depraved souls the aura is sometimes seen to glow with crimson-red shot through with black — the most vicious combination of evil known.

GREY

Grey is related to depression, gloom and sadness. A livid grey indicates fear. Grey people are plodders and often unimaginative. Grey-green indicates deceit and cunning.

BROWN

Dull red-brown like the colour of rust denotes avarice, and this may appear in the form of bars across the substance of the emotional body. Little more is said of brown, but its purer shades appear throughout nature in combination with green, giving a sense of stability.

ROSE PINK

This colour denotes refinement, modesty and a retiring nature. It is the colour of the emotional body and thus devotional attitudes, friendship and physical love. Rose pink acts upon the nervous system and helps to vitalize the etheric body by way of the emotional body, and disperse symptoms of debility. It increases the will to live.

These then are the basic colours which are seen in the aura; the interpretations are a guideline. Over the years a few people have made public what they could see in the aura; many, however, who cannot see, have taken the writings and utterances of those who could, and presented them again and again as accurate and factual. While in some instances the material may be correct, in others it may be completely erroneous. Colour interpretation requires great skill born of high sensitivity on all planes, and above all an inner knowledge based on fundamental principles and truth.

For the moment I would like to dwell on the subject of colour, and try to put the matter into perspective by looking very briefly at one or two deeper aspects which will help us to adopt a mental point of view of the subject rather than an emotional or astral one. Many people are familiar with the books that make the human aura sound like Piccadilly Circus or Times Square at night — a sea of flashing neon signs carrying subliminal messages — replete with passages that tell you if you have a dull throat chakra, and an even duller personality, then making love to a person with a nice bright blue throat will probably brighten your throat too and also do wonders by greening up your forehead, whatever that may mean. I'd like to emphasize that in order to really begin to understand colour in relationship to the esoteric constitution of man, his subtle bodies, the chakras and the planes of energy wherein he lives, it is essential to treat the subject seriously and make every effort to approach it from the higher mind.

Let us then return to the matter of blinds, the deliberate presentation of inaccurate information used by wise men through the ages to guard sacred and secret information. In her book *Letters on Occult Meditation*, Alice Bailey is quite open about the use of blinds, and she explains why they are used:

> I would here seek to put your mind at rest on the point as to whether the colours enumerated by me conflict with those enumerated by H.P.B. (Madame Blavatsky). You will not find they do, but both of us use blinds, and both of us use the same blinds as those who have eyes can see. A blind is not a blind when recognised, and I offer not the key. One or two hints I may give:—
>
> Complementary colours may be spoken of in occult books in terms of each other. Red may be called green and orange may be called blue. The key to the accurate interpretation of the term employed lies in the point of attainment of the unit under discussion. If speaking of the Ego (soul) one term may be used; if of the personality, another; whilst the Monad (spirit) or higher auric sphere may be described synthetically or in terms of the monadic ray.
>
> The colours of the higher or lower mind are at times spoken of in terms of the plane and not in terms of the ray involved.
>
> Blue-indigo, being cosmically related, and not simply analogous, may be used interchangeably for purposes of blinding.

Bailey then goes on to illustrate that indigo, blue, orange and yellow form a very complex relationship and are all used to describe a whole variety of aspects of one factor. She also points out that blinds are of great complexity, but for those with the seeing eye the choice of blinds is not arbitrary, but subject to rule and law. The true meanings of colour are not accessible to the emotional approach to knowledge, nor do they reveal themselves to the lower mind. The approach to the mystery of colour can only be made through the abstract or higher mind.

The colours we see as they manifest on the physical

plane reveal at this level their harshest qualities. On the emotional plane they take on a delicacy and beauty which is most captivating but in a deeper sense illusory. The colours of the astral plane are those so easily seen by the low-grade psychic. The interpretations we may receive from such sources are often very informative and interesting, but the question is, do they provide us with any real knowledge regarding the ultimate reality of our higher nature? I think not. Bailey states that:

> The very use of the word 'Colour' shews the intention, for, as you know, the definition of the word conveys the idea of concealment. Colour is therefore 'that which does conceal.' It is simply the objective medium by means of which the inner force transmits itself; it is the reflection upon matter of the type of influence that is emanating from the Logos, and which has penetrated to the densest part of His solar system. We recognize it as colour. The adept knows it as differentiated force, and the initiate of the higher degrees knows it as ultimate light, undifferentiated and undivided.

If we are serious in our study of colour and the aura, then our task must surely be to acknowledge the colours seen upon the lower planes and their reflections through the aura, but in so doing keep in mind that they are there to lead us beyond their beauty to the transformative and transmutative power of the Pure Light.

6

Sensing, seeing and reading the human aura

A person's aura tells a great deal about him.

Auras — Edgar Cayce

With few exceptions, most people would like to be able to see the human aura, and be gifted with the capacity to read and accurately interpret what they see. Few perhaps would consider just how much responsibility this capacity can carry with it, and just how much of a burden extended sight can bring. Of course it must have advantages when properly used, but consider for example what it must be like to have to cope with foreknowledge of death or disease among one's associates, friends or family. In his book, *A Door Marked Summer*, Michael Bentine relates how the faces of airmen who were shortly destined to die on bombing raids over Germany, during World War II, would take on the appearance of skulls to his inner sight; and more poignantly, the dramatic and frightening prevision of his son's coming death. It takes a particular quality of inner strength and a special philosophy of life to cope with such information in a balanced manner. Not too many people have such inner reserves, and the danger of precipitating anxiety states or being overwhelmed by extraneous data flooding in from prematurely opened psychic senses is a very real one.

We live in an era of high spiritual opportunity, a period perhaps unique in the long history of man. It is clearly a crisis point wherein a rapid expansion of consciousness on a mass scale is taking place. This period of high energy stimulation brings with it the potential for real growth, but it carries too the glamorous and illusory aspects to the forefront of awareness, which can deflect the individual temporarily from the straight and narrow path. Pop metaphysics offer enlightenment in ten easy lessons, or cosmic consciousness on a weekend workshop where half of the participants will be under the illusion that they have had a kundalini experience, after greening, blueing and brightening their chakras. Fortunately for most people the whole process turns out to be a ten minute wonder and they seldom succeed in raising, brightening, opening, or seeing anything.

At the risk of sounding rather sober, I think it is worthwhile sounding a note of caution with respect to exercises designed to make a spiritual superman out of you overnight. I have known personally two intelligent people, with a fair degree of knowledge in spiritual and religious matters, who experimented at length with rectal electrodes in order to raise kundalini. Fortunately they failed, and eventually one was found dead at the foot of a cliff, while the other learned to fly in a more orthodox manner and earned his pilot's licence.

Out of the few people who do persevere with certain types of mind-expanding and consciousness-enhancing exercises, a tiny minority may find that their developed gifts can be employed to serve others; but not a few become casualties of popularization, sometimes severely damaging their own psyches and most likely delaying their own spiritual evolvement. There is a popular misconception that to have extended vision is a mark of advanced spirituality. While this may be true in some instances, it is an erroneous assumption in the majority of cases. Aart Jurriaanse, who has done such a remarkable work of service by compiling extracts from Bailey's writings into specialized volumes, writes of the higher and lower psychism in his book, *Bridges — Basic Studies in Esoteric Philosophy*. Jurriaanse says of these:

> Psychic powers may either be related to egoic levels, and are then associated with soul qualities, or they may refer to the astral plane, in which case they will be characterised by illusion, glamour and distorting. For the sake of convenience these two aspects of psychism are referred to as 'higher' and 'lower' psychic powers.
>
> There is a tendency among esoteric students to condemn all sensitive response to psychic phenomena as retrogressive. In many instances this is true and may well lead to termination of the individual's spiritual development for that particular life span. On the other hand it may well be an indication of awakening spiritual sensitivity, and the first expression of such development. It is only when the psychic life is uncontrolled or over emphasised that it becomes undesirable, immersing the man in illusion and glamour. What is of importance is that the investigator of psychic phenomena should be focussed at least on the mental plane, but preferably he should work from the soul level.

Before embarking seriously on any exercises designed to enhance or develop the ability to see the aura, the first consideration is motive. Ask yourself why you want the ability. Is it for self-serving ends, or curiosity, or as a tool to be used in service to others? If it is the last then the chances of success are far greater in the long term, but discrimination should be employed in the choice of exercises. Be aware, too, that it takes time to enhance or develop sensitivity, and exercises have to be carried out regularly and systematically, possibly over long periods of time.

One of the most difficult barriers to overcome is the superficial and habitual use of our physical senses. They grip our awareness in a narrow vice-like grip, conditioning what we see or hear, dictating in many subtle ways just what we shall or shall not perceive. The very society we live in forms a conditioning of the senses, it tells us what we shall see, and how. If we are to learn to see the aura, then Don Juan's advice to Castaneda to look at the spaces between the leaves and foliage, not the form of the tree itself, becomes important. Our tendency is to look at the tree; to learn to see the aura you have to look at the spaces through and around objects. It really is a 180 degree turn with respect to the use of our physical sense of sight. We must look past the form to the essence.

All of us sense the aura. The terms good vibes and bad vibes, which have come into common usage, are indicative of this growing awareness and sensitivity. We know immediately when we feel uncomfortable in a certain place, or in the company of certain people. Terrifying events loaded with negative astral energies will imprint themselves into the physical fabric or space in the immediate area. One visit to the dungeons at the Tower of London will convince you of the reality of this. On the other hand we can be lifted into higher states of consciousness in some ancient churches or cathedrals, or at megalithic sites, where at certain times of the year the life-force pulsates in peculiar rhythm. The aura is revealed to us in these moments, but our tendency is to allow our physical senses to override the impressions flowing into our auras, and the intellect to supplant the intuition, by seeking rational and logical reasons for our feelings. The feeling aspect of the experience should be registered, but it is precisely here that we shut down the level of our perception, by exclaiming or thinking 'How beautiful!' or 'How lovely!' This is a sensory trap; we begin to add words, emotional words to an event in time and space that is in unceasing motion. We try to capture and hold with our senses, when we should be letting go and 'looking' at the spaces between the leaves and letting the event just happen. This is not a passive, open state in the astral sense, because this can be a dangerous inner posture to adopt, but a state of dynamic attention. Don Juan tells Castaneda that being a hunter means to see the world in a different way, and that the mood of the warrior calls for control over himself, and at the same time it calls for abandoning himself. It is a paradox, but when we set out to see the aura, we must be prepared to confront many such paradoxes.

Edgar Cayce felt that the majority of people do see the aura, but just do not realize it. Further, he believed that anyone can figure out what a person's aura looks like in a general way, by taking note of the colours that they employ and use in their homes and dress. You can follow changes in people's auras by observing how they change the colour combinations of their clothes from day to day. He writes:

How many times have you said of a woman, 'Why
does she wear that color? It does not suit her at all.'
How many times have you said 'How beautiful she
looks in that dress. The color is just right for her.
She was made to wear it.' In both cases you have been
reading an aura. The first woman was wearing a color
that clashed with her aura. The second woman was
wearing a color which harmonized with her aura.
All of you know what colors are helpful to your friends,
and bring out the best in them. They are the colors
that beat with the same vibration as the aura, and
thus strengthen and heighten it.

This passage illustrates perfectly what I have just said about paying attention to the essence behind the object. Everyone has experienced making such judgments about people's suitability of dress, but few if any would realize that such a conclusion is reached by unconsciously comparing the auric colours with the person's clothing. But this is precisely what has happened. We see the dress, and our perception at a conscious level stops right there. Logic and rationally conditioned processes of perception stop you dead in your tracks in an instant. If you want to read auras you will have to let your awareness flow past the form or objective aspect of the observation, and seek out the 'invisible' one that complements it and provides the real data from which your conclusion as to suitability of colour is really drawn. This is a basic exercise which will enable you to develop auric sight. It may be a little prosaic and lacking in glamour, but it is a practical exercise that can be initiated anytime and anywhere without any exotic preparations. You have a fertile world to draw experience from. Consider the conflicting colours worn by punks, extending even to greens and blues and reds in their hair. Tatty and deliberately torn clothing reflects a state, present in their auras, the matrix of which has been distorted by over-amplified rock music. Metal studded collars and jackets confer a state of hardness to the aura, a lack of pliability and a shutting down of sensitivity, which in some way might just be a reaction to the vast amount of sensory input that many young people seek today through Space Invader games, video films and discordant music. The skinhead is another example of our times who makes an interesting subject for aura study. He is often dressed in a plain shirt, open necked, sleeves rolled up to display the 'power symbols' of various tattoos on his arms and chest — birds of prey, dragons and daggers piercing hollow-eyed skulls. His jeans or trousers, with braces displayed, look as though they have had a row with his Dr Martin boots (the more lace holes the better). The bristling short haircut rounds out an auric picture of pure aggression and hardness.

In his little booklet on the aura, entitled *The Science of the Aura*, S.G. Ouseley has a chapter on developing auric sight in which he outlines a few basic exercises.

We will take a look at these because they are basic and they are simple. All of the exercises must be preceded by a period of relaxation in which we recollect that it is the 'spaces' we are to focus on and not the form.

The first exercise Ouseley recommends is that we seek to look at a magnet in as dark a room as possible. In fact he suggests that upon retiring you take a magnet to bed with you, and having placed yourself in a passive state, gaze at it as steadily as you can under the cover of the bedclothes. Within a short time you should see a faint glow shimmering around the two poles of the magnet. As you become more sensitive the faint glow will intensify into a bright white light with greens and blues merging into it. Sometimes ray-like projections of light become visible. The same process employing a quartz crystal will prove to be an interesting variation of this exercise. Von Reichenbach's sensitives reported beautiful streamers of colours issuing from the points of quartz crystals; veritable rainbows in fact appeared to flow around the crystals. As crystals can take up thought energies, and as pranic energies can be directed through them there must be many interesting variations on this exercise which can be devised to enhance auric sight.

The next exercise is best done with the hands held at a distance of about a foot from your eyes, fingers spread and tips touching. You may find it helpful if you first 'charge up' your hands by rubbing them briskly together. With your finger tips touching and against a background of dark material or a white wall in shadow, hold them together for a minute and concentrate on visualizing the energy flowing into your fingers. Then draw the fingers slowly apart keeping your eyes focused on the gradually widening gap. You will see radiations of energy issuing from your finger tips, spanning the gap between your two hands. Another way to build up a high charge of energy in the hands before looking at the finger tips is to hold them palms close to each other, and imagine the gap between them filling with energy, then move them slowly apart and together again in a gentle pulsing movement. As the energy charge builds you may feel tingling sensations in the palms of your hands, and eventually the charge can be so strong that it feels as though you are squeezing an invisible sponge. Then put the finger tips together and look for the auric radiations as you draw them apart.

Another exercise that Ouseley suggests is to work with a friend with whom you feel in harmony. A dark curtain or material should be hung on a wall opposite to a window. The subject then sits or stands before the dark material. If this work is being done during daylight hours, you should gaze at the sky for a half a minute or so. If the work is done at night then look at a lamp. Then sit down, close your eyes and relax and, if you are able, slip as quickly as possible into an alpha state. Concentrate your thoughts on seeing the aura in a gentle, unforced manner. Open your eyes and gaze at your subject and make a mental note of any field-like formations or lights around the body. You may not actually see anything, but the impression may come to you through feeling or sensing. For those who wish to work with this method on a regular basis, Roland Hunt, in his book *The Seven Keys to Colour Healing*, illustrates a muslin cabinet, with all the specifications. The advantages of such a cabinet is that it provides an area of softened light and promotes, as Hunt terms it, 'better diagnostic vision.'

It is useful to include a colour exercise. This can be carried out by placing slips of coloured paper in envelopes. Relax and enter into the alpha state; take several deep full yoga breaths. With each breath visualize one of the ray colours, taking each in turn. It is best to follow through the colours in a regular order. Ouseley suggests that the best way to do this is to visualize a globe of light, then 'see' each ray colour, begining with red and following through with blue, yellow, orange, green, violet and indigo.

After working through these colours for a while, pick up an envelope and place it against your forehead and try to receive the impression of the colour within.

These then are a few simple exercises which will help to unfold auric vision. Do not be discouraged if at first you do not have much success with them; the unfolding process takes time. In his booklet Ouseley sums this up very succinctly:

> With most people auric vision does not come in a few days or a few months. It is a life-time study and one's life and habits must be on a high plane to get good results. The finer forces are not discernible to the eyes of the gross materialist or the seekers after wonders and sensations. It is not to be considered that 'having eyes they see not.' The study and practice of seeing the aura is not to be lightly entered upon. It is a serious and priceless power and should be utilized for the uplift- ment and betterment of humanity.

While the exercises are useful, particularly the one that involves the direct observation of people and the colour and quality of their clothes, there are a number of other physical guides we can use which are a common everyday occurrence. For example, if you pause for a moment and consider how often you stop to scratch your face or body, you will realize that it is far more frequent than you had at first assumed. In fact you are probably scratching an itch right now, because your subconscious mind is trying to convey some data to you. These itches, when you know the significance of their varied locations, will prove to be a great aid in reading the aura. I call this the 'Itch-n-Scratch' aura reading technique. The past master of this technique is a man called Fred Kimball who lives in California. Kimball is a famous West Coast clairvoyant who came into prominence in the 1960s because of his ability to read the auras of animals. When doing readings for people he uses the itch-n-scratch method to aid him in pinpointing certain areas where help is needed, and as a guide to when certain events happened in the life of the person having a reading.

Kimball, an ex-merchant seaman who has travelled the world, and an ex-wrestler, was raised on a farm, and even as a young man he had an extraordinary rapport with animals. He has developed this gift into an uncanny ability to tune into an animal and in some manner elicit all kinds of information about its health, its homelife, what it gets to eat, if it likes its food, where it is allowed to go in the house and the areas that are taboo, what it thinks of its master or mistress and a whole variety of other bits and pieces about its life. To an onlooker these readings can become quite hilarious, as Kimball keeps up a constant two-way conversation while he works with the animal. The incongruous sight of Kimball sitting and having what appears to be a conversation with a dog is almost too much for some people, but the sobering thing is that what he relates in respect to the dog and all that goes on in its life, right down to the tiniest detail, is correct. Following a personal reading for a medical doctor friend of mine, Kimball offered to demonstrate his ability to read an animal's mind by tuning into the doctor's cat, six thousand miles away in England. He proceeded without any hesitation to outline where and when the cat was fed, what rooms it was allowed into and those that it wasn't, and what chairs it could sleep on. In passing he mentioned pictures on the walls and other various details. I had heard Kimball do this many times but my friend found it a staggering demonstration of clairvoyance. As we left he said, 'Well if I hadn't heard that with my own ears I wouldn't have believed it possible!'

Kimball's ability to read the minds and auras of human subjects is no less dramatic, and it is very practical in so far as he uses it to help people in such a way as to enable them to grasp the nature of their problems and then to do something about them. He teaches his method of aura reading in small classes and can rightly claim a high rate of success in helping people to develop their psychic abilities. Kimball has written a book on his methods called *The Language of ESP in Action*, some 206 pages long and filled with a lot of practical techniques. I will draw on some of this material in order to give some idea of his approach. Kimball writes:

The 'First Principle' of this system of inner communications is that the subconscious perceives data psychically and brings them to our attention as 'itches' in different parts of the body. When data are perceived psychically the sympathetic nervous system picks up the signals and carries them into the higher levels of conscious awareness.

The use of itches is not new of course; the Aboriginal uses a similar method of perception. Itches or pulsations in specific muscles indicate to him that a relative or friend is thinking of him and trying to get in touch. They may be many miles away, but the Aboriginal will go and sit quietly, or, if with a group, unobtrusively isolate himself until he has tuned into the source from where the impression is coming. The daily pressures of life that we are subjected to seldom allow such a procedure to be followed, even if we are alert enough to register such subtle impressions in the first place.

The next principle of Kimball's system is to divide the body in half. Any sensations or itches that occur on the left side refer to maleness and those on the right to femaleness. Kimball recognizes that there is a neural cross-over at the level of the neck and that the left side of the brain controls the right side of the body and vice versa; but for simplicity he just makes a straight division of it, while pointing out that now and then there are a few people who are left-handed and might cause you errors. Most left-handed people can be read as right-handed but it is important to determine this before the reading really gets under way. It is essential too that, when you read a person, you find out if you are picking up the other person in a straight or mirrored reaction. If you are a male reading a male, you check to see which side of the subject expresses authority; if it is the right side you will know that you are picking up impressions in the right side of your body from the right side of his. If it reverses, then the reverse is true.

Kimball points out that it is essential to do this work with a sense of fun, be enthusiastic and work in a state of calm and intense concentration. Sitting cold and reserved does not encourage the ESP function at all. When you have done some work congratulate yourself, give yourself a pat on the back, and ask your subconscious what to do to improve your performance next time. This will encourage growth and sensitivity. But if you clamp down and begin to get discouraged or critical then the subconscious will retreat. As Kimball says, validate your subconscious and be pleased with what it presents to you, and don't get discouraged at first, because it takes time to develop and control sensitivity.

Kimball states that Edgar Cayce taught that you can increase your ability to see auras by stimulating the nerves of your fingers by running the fingers of one hand over those of the other. Kimball does not seem too sure about the efficacy of this exercise and points out that we all have our own way of looking at auras if we will take the time to develop it. He instructs his students in the following manner:

To see an aura, look just past the person's head if you don't know how. As you look, you see out of the side of your eyes, it is like a distortion. Auras are just a distortion or an illusion on the side of the head. You may imagine you saw something, 'My eyes are playing tricks; they are just out of focus.' You look, see an aura and it is gone; this is the way they show up at the begining. Then I put my own color into this person's aura to brighten it up.

Normally I have the person sit down to see auras. Your eyes will seem as if they are playing tricks when you start. Look just past the person's head, not exactly. After you learn you can look at it directly. Look past the subject and you see a little distortion on the side.

Check yourself over before starting to read an aura. Become totally aware of your body — infections, injuries, pain, cool or hot, center heart, upper heart. Become totally aware. Start in usually with physical things and have the physical communications system set up the communication. Then move into the mental things and soon you are in emotional and spiritual communication.

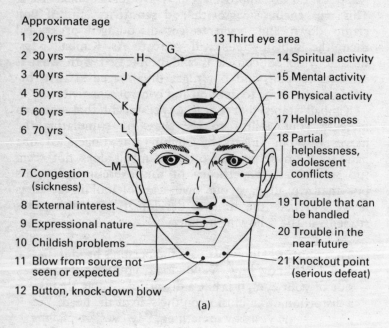

Approximate age

1 20 yrs
2 30 yrs
3 40 yrs
4 50 yrs
5 60 yrs
6 70 yrs

7 Congestion (sickness)
8 External interest
9 Expressional nature
10 Childish problems
11 Blow from source not seen or expected
12 Button, knock-down blow

G
H
J
K
L
M

13 Third eye area
14 Spiritual activity
15 Mental activity
16 Physical activity
17 Helplessness
18 Partial helplessness, adolescent conflicts
19 Trouble that can be handled
20 Trouble in the near future
21 Knockout point (serious defeat)

(a)

Figure 6.1 Kimball presents, in The Language of ESP in Action *a series of ten diagrams of the body showing itch points and their basic significance. The text elaborates on each of these in detail*

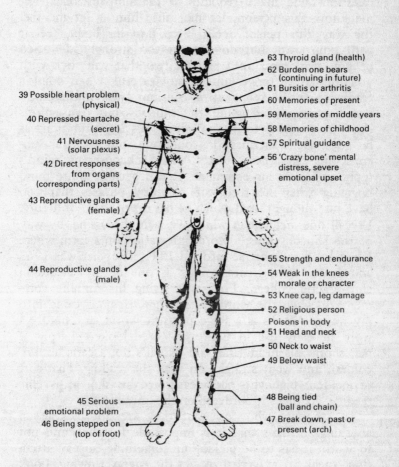

39 Possible heart problem (physical)

40 Repressed heartache (secret)

41 Nervousness (solar plexus)

42 Direct responses from organs (corresponding parts)

43 Reproductive glands (female)

44 Reproductive glands (male)

45 Serious emotional problem

46 Being stepped on (top of foot)

63 Thyroid gland (health)

62 Burden one bears (continuing in future)

61 Bursitis or arthritis

60 Memories of present

59 Memories of middle years

58 Memories of childhood

57 Spiritual guidance

56 'Crazy bone' mental distress, severe emotional upset

55 Strength and endurance

54 Weak in the knees morale or character

53 Knee cap, leg damage

52 Religious person
Poisons in body

51 Head and neck

50 Neck to waist

49 Below waist

48 Being tied (ball and chain)

47 Break down, past or present (arch)

and makes an excellent guide for reading the aura (a) Some of the itch points on the head and face (b) Front view of the body showing itch points

Kimball says when looking at a person to see his aura, talk to yourself; say 'Let me see this person's aura and let me feel with him.' You may get pains and itches as your subconscious directs you where to look. Constantly ask questions and make requests to the subconscious: 'Let me know this person, let me sense him — let me feel the way this person feels.' Step into his body, feel it with your own, but do not get too strongly identified or you may pick up a pain or two that will stick with you for days after if you are not careful. When doing a reading Kimball keeps up a constant two- or three-way conversation, bringing all the subconscious transactions out into a verbal form and adding his interpretations as he goes. He asks questions out loud, but to your subconscious; he then relates your subconscious mind's reply and gives his comment. It can become quite mind boggling when he reels off technical phrases that you have just thought, and which he has never heard of before. I recall one incident in which we were discussing, by way of the subconscious, a worm infestation on a farm where I had lived in Somerset around 1941. The year was 1963 and I was taking parasitology as one of my classes in chiropractic college. Fred was giving his running commentary when the words *ascaris lumbricoides* came into my mind. Ascaris is a large parasitic worm, and hardly a word in daily use in California. Fred looked sharply at me, shook his head, and said 'No it's not ascaris lumbricoides', and went straight on with the reading. That sort of incident highlights the measure of his skill in psychic reading. At times it bordered on the uncanny.

To students who feel that they are not picking up anything, he says that it is impossible for the mind not to work; it has to be picking up something, so pay attention, speak to it, verbalize, get the energy flowing. Look at a person, look for the colours that are a part of that person, see the haze around the body, ask your mind what is emerging from that haze, what colours are showing up.

Gradually, as you work in this manner and learn to look past the form to the essence, images and impressions will begin to register with more clarity. You may not see colours around the person, but in your mind's eye. Acknowledge them, say thank you to your subconscious and let the flow of data bearing energy run its course. Above all work in a state of relaxed attention and with enthusiasm.

Seeing the aura clairvoyantly is just one way of working. There are other approaches open which may prove more suitable to some individuals. If your sense of touch is sensitive then you may find that you can scan the aura by hand and pick up information in this manner. Brugh Joy has taught many people how to use this technique to great advantage and in his book *Joy's Way* he gives detailed instructions and exercises for developing this gift. Body-energy fields can stimulate a variety of sensory systems in the hands: pressure receptors, heat receptors and receptors for cold, light touch, pain and vibratory energies. All of these come into play at one time or another when scanning body-energy fields. Joy outlines the following requisites for successful hand scanning:

1 Be totally receptive with consciousness focused in your hands.
2 Don't project what you think should be there into the space between you and the subject.
3 The detector hand must be held relaxed, fingers bent and slightly apart. A rigid hand is not a good detector.
4 Have your sleeves rolled up, as the forearm can pick up energy fields as well.
5 Explore to see if you are more sensitive scanning with your right or left hand.
6 Scan slowly so that energy impressions can be registered by the mind, there is a lag between the receptor registering the energy in the field and the stimulus reaching the brain.

7 If the hand becomes 'overcharged' during scanning, then rest it or flick the charge from the hands.

8 Don't *try* to feel the fields, simply *allow* them to enter into your awareness.

9 Scan eight to twelve inches from the body. Jewelry and heavy belt buckles should be removed from the subject.

10 Subject must be in a relaxed state, resting, feet approximately twelve inches apart. Silence should be observed during scanning.

11 Feel the subject's pulse using the three finger method. This facilitates tuning into them.

12 Begin by scanning the large chest and abdominal areas. Keep the hands moving slowly as it is through the contrast of moving through various aspects of the field that you register the differences.

As with all other methods of 'reading' the aura, hand scanning takes time to develop. Don't overdo the early sessions or you will fatigue your subtle sense of touch and quite likely deplete your own energy-fields. By way of encouragement, Joy points out that less than one per cent of people are totally unable to detect body energy-fields by hand scanning, so don't give up or be discouraged in your first phase of exploratory work.

Heat and cold are probably the easiest sensations to pick up, and you have to be careful that these are not actually physical in origin. So when scanning the face, for example, you should ask your subject to hold his breath for a moment or two. Sensations registered through hand scanning will take many forms: heat and cold, as previously mentioned, tingling, clamminess, lightness and vitality. Some people have an energy-field that feels tacky and your hands seem to stick to it; sometimes such a field can impart the most unpleasant sensations to your hands. When this happens quickly shake them and flick any effluvia from them. Following any hand scanning session it is advisable to wash your hands and forearms with cold running water. To clear your aura entirely you should let the tap run and, cupping your washed hands around and about three inches from the flow, step backwards and with each step move your hands further apart, but keeping them cupped as if around the water. Move back until your arms are outstretched sideways, then advance towards the water reversing the whole procedure.

Just as the observation of people's clothes can give us practical information regarding their aura, there is another common everyday experience which may in some indirect manner help us to come to a wider understanding of the aura, and enhance our inner sensitivity. If you look at a dew drop in the early morning sunlight and then half close your eyes, so that your eyelashes partly cover your field of vision, you will see hundreds of tiny lines of brilliant light emerging from the dew drop. The more you close the space you are looking out through, the longer the lines of light get. As you open your eyes, they shorten and withdraw into the dew drop again. It can be quite entertaining and absorbing to keep on lengthening and shortening these lines of light. If there is no dew drop handy then look at a candle flame in a darkened room and you will get a similar effect. 'So what?' you might say, everyone knows this phenomenon and has at some time or another tried it. It is curious how we dismiss such an experience as a purely physical event. We seldom stop and question such things nor do we follow them through with concentrated attention. I have certainly done what most people would do, squinted a few times at the source of light, played with the lines for a moment or two and then dismissed the matter.

This phenomenon which we dismiss so lightly has been observed and commented upon by certain Sufi mystics, who seem to feel it has significance of some spiritual import. We will return to them in a moment, after we look at the observations recorded by Jurij Moskvitin in his book *Essay on the Origin of Thought*, published by Ohio University Press in 1974. Moskvitin records that he watched the colours of the spectrum through half-closed eyes, just like most of us have, when suddenly he became aware of a mosaic-like background that was constantly changing and moving. Sometimes it looked like layers of screens, one behind another. On these screens various patterns appeared, taking the form of swastikas and triangles and various other shapes. Many of them he recognized as symbols from religious art, some stylized like Mexican masks. Amongst these forms danced brilliant sparks of light with tiny tails attached to them. He writes: 'The forms came floating out of anything I looked at, lying like cobwebs around all objects, and from these stretching into my eyes, as if the objects emanated from me.' The dots that Moskvitin observes sound very much like the orgone dots of Reich, or the vitality globules of theosophical literature. These, as we have seen, are an aspect of the pranic forces wherein all forms have their origins, according to the Vedas. The cobweb-like fields he sees around objects sound like a poetic description of the aura. Perhaps Moskvitin was psychic and did not recognize the fact, or perhaps he just took a little more time to observe what he saw, and through concentration actually began to penetrate deeper into the spectrum of colours reflected in the lines of light. If the latter is true then we can all benefit from such an exercise if we wish to enhance our sensitivity.

The great Sufi philosopher and mystic Muhyiddin Ibn 'Arabi writes in the Sufi texts of the Earth of True Reality, mentioning the strange and wondrous marvels it contains. A multitude of things exist on that Earth which are rationally impossible, and which logic has shown are not compatible with reality as we know it. However, many visionary mystics confirm the existence of this Earth and all it holds. In all the universes of this Earth it is said that there is one especially created in our image where our homologue lives. The palm tree is the leitmotiv of the celestial Earth, having been fashioned from a speck of clay left over after God had moulded the forms of Adam and the subtle form of the subtle Earth or mystic Eve. That speck of clay is symbolic of the point of consciousness where one gains access to the celestial Earth. The limitless expanse of the celestial Earth begins at the point where the directions of sensory space end. It is at this point where we step into the separate reality of Don Juan; it is here in this peculiar balance point of awareness that we 'see' the aura, where the sensory world meets the subtle world. Here is the 'space between the leaves' that reveals another world.

In *Spiritual Body and Celestial Earth* Henry Corbin writes:

> In that Earth there are gardens, paradises, animals, minerals — God alone can know how many. Now, everything that is to be found on that Earth, absolutely everything, is alive and speaks, has a life analogous to that of every living being endowed with thought and speech. Endowed with thought and speech, the beings there correspond to what they are here below, with the difference that in that celestial Earth things are permanent, imperishable, unchangeable; their universe does not die.

Corbin goes on to say that our physical bodies do not have access to this world, and so it is that the mystics in their subtle bodies travel there and report on the wonders they see. There are dwellers in this paradise who watch for us to approach the gates, and whenever one of us seeks the way of access to that Earth, one of them hastens towards us — an ally of immeasurable benevolence. We ourselves are a part of the celestial Earth and our homologue there is a body of light fibres with subtle tenuous prolongations that extend to the borders of the Earth. Corbin suggests how we can visualize the point of entry into the separate reality of the celestial Earth, and you will see just what Jurij Moskvitin came upon as he lay on his back in the sun and began to gaze through half-closed eyes. Whether he was aware of the writings of the Sufi mystics I do not know; it is not important. What matters is that we have an exercise enfolded in this process that is of real import, not only in helping us to 'see' the aura, but in having the potential to shift the whole focus of how we see. It brings us to the 'Point of Power' that Seth in the writings of Jane Roberts speaks about — the moment in time which is a gate that leads you out of time. Let us see what Corbin has to say.

> To give a picture which will help you to grasp how it is that that Earth can extend as far as our world, I suggest the following comparison. Suppose a man fixes his gaze on a lamp, or on the sun, or the moon, and then half shuts his eyes so that his eyelashes veil the luminous body from his gaze; then he will see something like a multitude of lines of light stretching from the luminous body to his eyes — a whole network starting from the lamp, for example, and reaching right to his own eyes. When the eyelids are slowly and gradually raised, the observer sees the network of lines of light draw back little by little and gather into the luminous body.
>
> And so the luminous body is analogous here to the location especially reserved in that Earth for such and such a form of apparition (a subtle body clothing a spiritual entity). The observer in this case represents our own world. As for the expansion of the lines of light, this corresponds to the forms of the subtle bodies in which our souls are transported to the threshold of Paradise during sleep and after death.

Corbin continues to expand on this theme by saying that your effort to see the lines of light is analogous to the capacity for visionary apperception. As you look through lowered eyelashes the emission of the lines of light from the dew drop or lamp corresponds to the emissions of the subtle bodies when you have attained the ability to 'see' the other reality. And, finally, the retraction of the lines of light, as you open your eyes slowly, represents the return of the subtle forms withdrawing into the celestial Earth when your capacity to perceive them ceases. Corbin ends by saying 'There is no explanation beyond this explanation.' In other words do not pursue these ideas with your intellect and logic, but let the right brain mode of perception take over. Put aside your conditioned response to the forms of the physical world and look beyond them. In time you will develop the capacity to see.

7

Dowsing and the human aura

In recent times, the principles of dowsing have been used to seek out the invisible and unknown in other fields, particularly in medicine.

The Divination of Disease — Dr H. Tomlinson

Dowsing as a means of divination has been employed by man for many centuries for detecting various hidden things. Mostly it has been used to locate sources of water for human and animal consumption, but it is by no means limited to such a use. Today dowsers look for oil, minerals, missing persons and lost objects. Lay people use it to determine what foods suit them best, doctors employ pendulum diagnosis to help them in their practices, and to select remedies. Archeologists dowse out hidden burial sites and explore the web of ley lines that criss-cross the British countryside. As Tom Graves says in his excellent book *Dowsing*:

Dowsing is more than a subject, it's a skill, a tool — one which I suppose can be used to tackle any problem you care to name. In another sense it's not so much a subject as a specific state of mind: it's a mental tool, in that it appears to be an analytical tool which uses

intuition, an intuitive tool based on analysis, and both
of these put together — a paradoxical mental tool!

Certainly dowsing is a first class way to explore the subtle
anatomy of man, his chakras and the aura. It is a tool with
a potential limited only by the sensitivity and knowledge
of the dowser, and it provides us with yet another way
we can develop our skills in the field of aura exploration.
The tools are simple enough, a couple of angle rods made
out of old wire coat hangers or a simple pendulum bob on
a thread.

As dowsing is nothing more nor less than the detection
of energy fields, it can readily be employed to map out
the human aura. We will get on with the practical aspects
of this in a moment, but first it is well worthwhile taking
a look at the work of one or two pioneers in this field,
and observe their different approaches. In 1925 the
Reverend Verne Cameron, who then owned some land
near Escondido in Southern California, was faced with the
problem of finding a source of water. He had sunk a shaft
on the site of an existing spring but unfortunately this did
not increase his water supply. A neighbour offered to help
Cameron and brought a dowsing device made up of coil
springs attached to a wire loop. They found water and
the incident set the good Reverend to exploring the
dowsing phenomenon. He made a whole series of detection
instruments, some quite complex with rotating dials and
quartz jewel bearings, and others so bulky as to be imprac-
tical. One of Cameron's simpler dowsing devices was the
Aurameter, which is a horizontal pendulum consisting of
a metal tubular handle with a wire extending from it that
has a weight at the end and a cylindrical spring near the
handle. The purpose of the spring, according to Cameron,
is to select and amplify the periodic oscillations of the
dowser's muscles in response to the energies being sought
with the pendulum. The instrument is held firmly but not
too tightly with the weighted point directed at the person

whose aura is to be mapped. As the tip touches upon the field it begins to move in a series of circular or elliptical movements, indicating the presence of the aura. A similar and far less sophisticated device is the amplifying pendulum of Pasquini, which will serve any beginner in this method of aura mapping just as well as the Aurameter, and it is much cheaper to purchase.

Cameron has some good advice to give regarding the use of the Aurameter. He says to be sure to visualize the instrument as an extension of your own body, complete with nerves from which its messages can be sent to your consciousness. He uses the analogy of the relationship between a good driver and his car: they become one, each an extension of the other. An accomplished radiesthetist (dowser), he points out, should be able to feel the instrument and its reactions amidst the various energy fields, and likewise to be with it. Then he gives the most important piece of advice it is possible to give to any neophyte dowser.

> Cultivate an impartial, non-interested outlook; be a 'disinterested onlooker' cataloguing but not reacting to the messages the instrument gives. If you use the instrument with too-strong a desire to find or to gain data then you will create the data desired but with the usual errors of the human consciousness when it is restricted by bias and prejudice.

Having noted the Reverend Verne Cameron's advice about not letting your own concepts and beliefs interfere with what you are searching out, or indeed literally creating thoughtforms by anticipation, a quick look at his mapped outline of the human aura will suggest that he appears not to have taken his own advice. He agrees that there are three bands to the aura, but cuts them off short at the neck, which differs from the findings of other investigators and indeed clairvoyants. Then lo and behold! in the Christian tradition his male figure sprouts wings and a halo in his aura, and what looks like navigational devices for use when passing through subtle terrain — a head fin for stabilization and a concentration beam as a contour sensor, no less! The diagram illustrates the great differences between Cameron's findings, which I firmly believe are heavily influenced by his subconscious, and those of Kilner who was far more objective in his approach. There is a lesson here, and it is that you will find what you expect to find, if you expect it hard enough. When dowsing the aura, be centred, be calm, be enthusiastic, but above all be open and free from expectation and do not project images onto your subject or you will read them back to yourself and learn little or nothing about the aura.

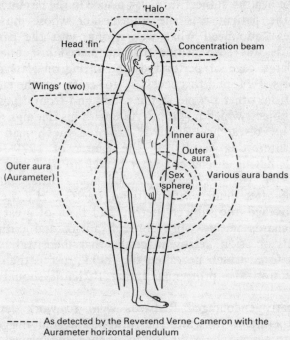

- - - - - As detected by the Reverend Verne Cameron with the Aurameter horizontal pendulum

────── As seen through Kilner Screens

Figure 7.1 Aura of a healthy male subject

During the 1920s a brilliant English physician by the name of Guyon Richards incorporated dowsing into his practice to diagnose disease and to select more accurately the appropriate medicines for his patients. He soon moved away from the simple pendulum to a fairly complex electrical apparatus based on an American device developed in the early 1900s called an Osciloclast. The purpose of this instrument was to detect the same energies picked up by the dowser, but to render these energies measurable in electrical terms (ohms) and to be able to quantify the findings. Guyon Richards felt that the patient's body was a transmitting station; the wires attaching the patient to the instrument, the aerial; the valve sets, an amplifier; and the healthy subject who was placed in the circuit along with the patient was the loudspeaker whose muscular reflexes announced what was wrong with the patient. Richards was so sensitive that he placed his apparatus in a large cage of perforated zinc sitting on glass piano supports. He found this necessary to screen out the emanations from other people in the room, and from drugs and other objects which might interfere with his findings.

In his researches Richards explored the human aura with interesting results. In the winter of 1929-30 he records having discovered what he felt to be a new form of matter. His discoveries puzzled him a little, and one evening after dinner with a friend, one Col. H.P. Lefroy, he broached the subject. Lefroy had been of great help to Richards in his work through advice and criticism. On this occasion Lefroy suggested that there was a unit of life-force which he called the 'bion', just as there was an electron and proton, and that Richards should find it.

Greatly encouraged Richards went to work devising an experiment in which he wrapped a gold nugget in lead, this again he wrapped in copper and placed in a tin box. This package was connected to his detecting device but no reaction could be obtained to gold. He then tried to get reactions to lead and copper in turn and failed. He then tuned his instrument to tin and got a good reaction. Leaving the dial tuning for tin on the first rheostat, Richards tuned the next one to copper and got a reaction. He then repeated this process for lead and gold on successive rheostats and got clear reactions. This gave him the clue to the energy structures he called biomorphs: they were formed of successive shells of energy. He found every life-form had these biomorph shells which seemed to increase on an ascending evolutionary scale, for example:

Minerals: one-ring biomorphs
Vegetables: two-ring biomorphs
Insects and reptiles: three-ring biomorphs
Mammals and birds: three- and four-ring biomorphs
Man: four- and five-ring biomorphs

Richards found that when he came to study the aura, similar bands of frequencies were found to surround the body. This suggested to him that Darwin's general idea of evolution was true. He found that over the pregnant uterus in the early months he was able to detect the reptilian form of the biomorph and later the mammalian before the human form arrived with its four or five rings. In his book, *The Chain of Life*, Richards wrote:

You can, if you please, think that each form arrived by a special act of creation. In a sense this must of necessity be so, for if the universe is the thought of God, the Great Architect, the added form of life arrived by His thought when the time was ripe for its arrival. It was doubtless in His thought when from the beginning of time predetermined for our planet, and the question whether things grew by themselves from a primordial stimulus, or by an ever-present thought and care, is a matter of temperament of the thinker.

In the eternal I conceive there can be no beginning or end, but constant being, so with His creation of thought.

> Creative power goes on all the time. The question
> of growth versus creation seems really futile.

Richards applied the biomorphic principle to his aura research and found that it consisted of five layers and a narrow circlet which lay between the first two rings. By applying various colours to the aura he discovered that it intensified the field. This is interesting particularly in view of one of the techniques used by Fred Kimball in reading the aura. Kimball projects colour mentally onto the aura of the sitter in order to intensify their colours and thus facilitate the reading.

Richards found that the fifth ring of the human aura gave rise to a variety of phenomena. In health the individual had a personal colour, and in disease a colour corresponding to the imbalance. By detecting these colours and then using the services of a friend who was clairvoyant, Richards confirmed his findings again and again. The aura changes in disease in two ways: there is an alteration in the widths of the bands and the frequency changes. In cancer, Richards reported that the third layer is reduced from four inches to as little as half an inch, and the intensity from 111,111 ohms to as low as 11 ohms. During sleep, in trance, or under anaesthetic, the aura loses its three outer layers.

In his practice Richards used auric frequencies for the final test as to suitability of drugs, vaccines, colours, or glandular extracts. Testing various homoeopathic potencies and colour he got the following alterations to the aura of his subject. The greatest expansions of the field occurred when endocrine gland potencies were taken, which is perhaps not surprising in view of their relationship to the chakras. This mode of testing involved a shielded neon lamp held to the subject's aura. The observer holding the light backs away until the lamp goes out; this point indicates the outer edge of the aura. The subject stands, for the purposes of this test, upon a grounded metal plate that is charged to a high voltage; this provides the energy to illuminate the neon light by exciting the auric field of the subject, but, according to Richards, not expanding it. The results from these tests were as given in Table 7.1:

Table 7.1

Distance before dose (inches)		Dose given	Distance afterwards (inches)
1	38	Orchitic 100c	45
2	50	Colour red	56
3	43	Orchitic 100c	59
4	38	Aluminium 30c	42
5	32	Strep. vaccine	41
6	35	Coli vaccine	38

Tests indicated too that there were life-force centres connected to the aura. These are similar in concept to the chakras, and one of these centres near the episternal notch has a close connection to the disease cancer, although is not confined to it. Deep emotional problems involve a centre over the sternum and this often involves the spleen and sex centres, according to Richards.

In his work he was meticulous and took no one else's word for anything, and the result is a unique body of evidence and research material. Colour and the effects it had on the aura did not slip his attention, and, not content with researching this area in relationship to man alone, he dealt with the other kingdoms in nature as well. Worms, minerals, plants and even a bull terrier came under his scrutiny. Richards found layers of colour in the human aura going out as far as ten feet. Table 7.2 outlines his findings and may be useful as a guide to further exploration. Richards points out that to clairvoyant sight his own aura extended through the visible spectrum from red to green, and a clairvoyant associate's from violet to yellow. This being the case, he demures

Table 7.2

Blue	½"
Yellow	⅛"
Red	4"
Orange	4"
Yellow	4"
Red Orange Yellow Green Blue Violet	Covering 3½"
Ultra-violet	17" to 83"
Blue	83" to 94"
Yellow streamers	from body to 10 feet

from putting too much stock in reading a subject's character from the aura, and points out that until a great deal of
work is done he is sceptical about any claims about character readings from aura colours *by any set rules* (my italics).
He concludes his observations on his researches into the
aura by saying:

> Whatever the nature of the outer aura may be, our
> subject or detector is also human, and has in his body
> and aura similar frequencies to those of the person we
> are studying. Proof, therefore, one way or the other is
> difficult. We can only make deductions which are sure
> to be coloured by our mental attitude. The safest plan
> is to record observations and go on making them till
> further evidence is obtained and the subject better
> understood. The one thing the researcher must not do
> is to let the thought 'impossible' enter his mind.

Sage advice from a remarkably perceptive physician. To
anyone who enters the field of dowsing in general and
researching the human aura in particular, it is of paramount importance to keep an open mind, record in detail

what you find, no matter how unusual it may seem, and to keep on piling up data. Thus will your sensitivity be enhanced and your expertise sharpened.

Let us return now to the tools used in aura dowsing, the angle rods made from old wire coat hangers and the pendulum. The angle rod should have about a five inch handle, and the rest of the wire cut off at the curve of the hanger serves as the detecting probe. The handle should be placed in a metal tube or hollow wooden dowel so that it can swing freely. To read or detect the aura stand in a relaxed state of body and mind with your hands at your sides, rods pointing to the ground. As you raise them up to waist level with your elbows loosely at your sides, look directly at your subject. Be sure that you are a suitable distance from him, say eight to ten feet. Then holding the mental concept of the outer edge of the aura clearly in thought, walk slowly towards him. As the rods pick up the distal edge of his aura they will cross over each other. You can then step backwards and the rods will resume their former position of a body-width apart. Move forward again and register the outer edge of the aura again, and now instead of stepping back, think of the second layer of the aura and the rods will swing apart. Now holding that thought move forward again and as you reach the second layer the rods will cross. In this manner each layer of the aura can be detected and measured before you record your findings in a notebook kept especially for the purpose.

This simple process can be applied to all aura mapping, but it is essential to have clear, precise thought patterns if you want clear answers. The same applies when looking for the predominant colour in each layer of the aura. You can hold the colour in mind or put a sample of it in one of your hands; the latter is known as a 'witness' and can in fact be anything you may be searching for. Providing you are careful to select the right colour for a person, you can experiment by mentally projecting that colour into his aura, and then measuring the layers to see if they have expanded. Once again note your results. You may find it a good idea to note the conditions under which the aura mapping is taking place: indoors or outdoors, the weather conditions, the state of your subject's health, and so on. One of the most famous dowsers of all times was the Abbé Mermet, a Catholic priest. Using a detailed scale map of an area in South America, he sat in his study in Switzerland and dowsed the precise location to put down a bore hole for water. He then added that the drillers would have to contend with certain geological strata, the depths of each of which he gave details about. He predicted the flow in gallons per minute, its potability and temperature. He was correct in every detail. For amusement sometimes he would count the number of cars crossing a certain bridge in Paris from the comfort of his study. On a more serious note he found missing persons or located bodies of murder victims for the police. On one occasion he went out with a group of school children to demonstrate the wonders of dowsing, and try as he might he could get no reaction at all with his pendulum. He apologized and told the children that this sort of experience was most unusual and that there must be some sort of calamity in the world. It turned out that a tidal wave had just hit Japan killing many people. This illustrates, I believe, the need to make brief notes about conditions and locations when mapping the aura, because we are all connected at the higher levels and we must be aware of the implications and effect of this fact.

Just as the Abbé Mermet and, in fact, thousands of other dowsers have done distant detection with a pendulum, you can map the aura of a person from his photograph. For this purpose you need a fine pointed pendulum and a twelve inch ruler. Place the subject's photo at the left-hand end of the ruler, and, using a scale of one inch to a foot, you can begin by tuning in the pendulum over the photograph. It will usually swing in a clockwise direction. Having tuned in, you then mentally ask for the point on the rule which represents the outer edge of the aura, and as you hold this thought move your pendulum away from the photo along the rule. When it detects this point you should feel a drag on the pendulum as you pass it and it will begin to swing back towards the point. By moving the pendulum carefully up and down the rule in this area you will pin-point the exact position of the outer edges of the aura. When initially moving your pendulum from the photo and along the rule it is best to let it beat across the rule at right angles to it, rather than allowing it to continue the circular movement from tuning. With some ingenuity you can dowse out the auric fields, their dominant colours, the states of the chakras, and the general health pattern of your subject.

When working directly with your subject, it is important to learn to become sensitive to the various gradients or qualities of energy you encounter with the rods or pendulum. The same thing, you may recall, applied to hand scanning. Dowsing the aura is the same as hand scanning in a sense, but you have the added benefit of a responsive detector in the form of rods or a pendulum. These will react where you may not actually register any energies through hand scanning. The same rules of application suit each approach: be relaxed and attentive and do not feed expectation into the field of operation.

You may wonder if there are any dangers in this form of energy field exploration. The answer, in short, has to be yes! Whenever two life-fields interact there is a potential danger that data in the form of imbalances will find their way from one field to the other, and this is especially true if one of the people involved is highly neurotic. Often people with highly sensitive natures are drawn almost irresistibly into dowsing, and they find that they are as a rule quite adept at it. If these people have a volatile emotional nature, they will in all probability end up in an acute state of anxiety if they do too much of this kind of work. The time to quit in such cases is before God starts giving instructions through the pendulum, and I have known people who have believed this to be true in their cases. A common sense attitude, with an open mind and your feet firmly planted on the ground, is the best posture to adopt and maintain in this work.

For the practical ins and outs of dowsing, there are no better books than *Dowsing* by Tom Graves, and *Divining the Primary Sense* by Herbert Weaver. These will give you a thorough grounding upon which to base your own researches.

In closing this chapter I would like to say that dowsing offers one of the simplest and easiest approaches to 'seeing' the aura. As I said earlier, the only limitations are your own depth of sensitivity and the knowledge you have of the subject. Divination by these means has been used by shamans down the ages. Perhaps we can add to our self-knowledge through dowsing, and, when competent, employ it to help others.

8

Auric pollution – physical and psychic

The aura is a combination of radiations, energies and arranged forces, which can either attract or repel the good or the bad, and it is through contacts thus effected that the whole trend of a man's life will be determined.

Bridges – Aart Jurriaanse

The human aura has a magnetic quality about it, attracting and repelling various energies. It soaks up a continual flow of impressions from the physical, emotional and mental worlds, much of it little more than psychic static. This attraction is qualified and conditioned by our state of mind, the general trend of our emotions and the way we nourish and look after our physical body. The continual chatter of the mind keeps the aura filled with incomplete and hazy thoughtforms, and to these are added emotional currents of energy which tend to reinforce half-formed thoughts. In this fluctuating undertow of dissonant energies, resentments flare up as harsh colours. Imagined slights become the focus of mental-emotional scenarios, and we construct a world around us in this manner that can become filled with menace, anxiety and stress. The aura then reflects a confused chaos of agitated colours, swirling here and there, pulled by one emotion or uncontrolled thought after another. In this state, which is the lot of many people today, the aura becomes devitalized and thus open to invasive influences that are far from beneficial. If unchecked, these inimical influences can lead to depressive states and neurotic patterns of behaviour which render the individual ineffective, and generally destroy the joy and wonder that life should bring.

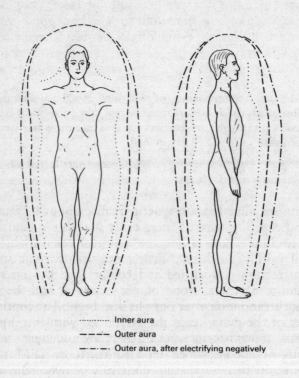

.... Inner aura
— — — Outer aura
—·—·— Outer aura, after electrifying negatively

Figure 8.1 Illustration by Kilner of the effect of negatively electrifying aura, causing the outer shell to expand

The sages of old were very aware of the human condition of semi-blindness, but one doubts if even they could have foreseen the pressures and stresses that modern man has to contend with. Centuries ago stresses were local; now they impinge on a global scale and everyone is subjected to them through the media, which continually emphasize the negative aspects of what is going on in the world. What amounts to a continuous bombardment of socially and economically threatening events flows from newspapers, radios and television twenty-four hours a day into the aura of the individual and humanity at large. Few escape this conditioning, which moulds the thinking processes and emotional responses of millions of people. The media set one nation against another, and political broadcasts manipulate the emotional bodies of countless people, creating fear and divisive attitudes.

The media are used to create desire for material things, and subliminal techniques are employed on television and in advertisements in the glossy magazines. Just to look at a television screen induces a form of light hypnotic trance because the fine flickering lines of the picture on the tube entrain the mind, leaving it passive and wide open to suggestion. The advertising world is of course well aware of this phenomenon and how to exploit it and you into the bargain. Basically all advertising is aimed at the astral or emotional body, its function being to stir up desire. To this may be added a slick presentation that will appeal to the lower-mind and touch upon the mental aura. To add power to these images music is added, and in order to punch the message past any discriminating faculty you may have, points of light will flash or scintillate, images will flicker at a certain speed or scenes will be rapidly shifted back and forth from one view to another. These devices are subliminal and designed to overcome your resistance, if indeed you have any, to certain ideas, certain products and indeed certain politicians. The next time you see a flashing point of light on a television advertisement, or a point of light that scintillates accompanied by a single pinging note of music, please remember that the advertiser has just implanted what amounts to a directive in your subconscious mind; he has polluted your aura with junk energy. Junk foods we are very aware of today; junk energy implants are a more recent concept and far more insidious in their influence upon your aura and subsequently your life.

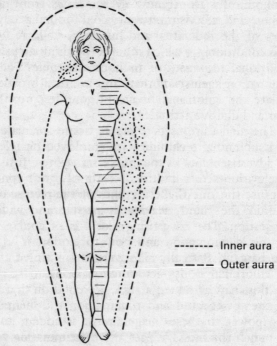

-------- Inner aura
------- Outer aura

Figure 8.2 Pathological appearance of aura as seen through the Kilner Screen. Granular textures and holes appear in the auric field

Let us have a closer look at the influence of television upon the aura, bearing in mind that it now has the added power of colour which increases its attraction potential a hundredfold. In her book *The Plug-In Drug*, Marie Winn carefully documents the insidious effects that prolonged viewing of television can have, not only on children but on adults also. First of all it has a hypnotic effect, so much so that children who watch up to thirty hours a week sometimes reach such a state of trance that their attention cannot be claimed, even when shouted out. The only way they snap out of it is when the set is switched off. A lot of energy, apart from harmful radiations, comes out of the TV screen, and is passively soaked up. This destroys initiative and creates irritability in many children, who often become quite violent when the set is switched off, in an unconscious attempt to discharge the energy. The passivity induced by television viewing is used by advertisers to plant their messages and feed desires deep in the subconscious. Addiction to television is a recognized syndrome, and people in foreign countries who are vacationing or passing through will quite cheerfully watch programmes in languages they cannot understand a word of, so obsessive is the power of 'the box'. It has been suggested that the fast shifting of the visual frames in television is related to the hyperkinetic syndrome in children which is rapidly increasing in the modern world. Winn's book is a frightening document, and when we consider the way that the subconscious can be manipulated by this aspect of the media, you may begin to wonder just which thoughts and opinions are your own, and what effects the negative news and violence have upon your mind and auric fields.

Right in the same league with television are the slick advertisements in the glossy magazines. Many of those advertisements of products used by most people contain subliminal messages. These are developed by the juxtaposition of various components of the picture or by drawing and air-brushing in words and symbols. Dr Wilson Bryan Key, author of a best selling book, *Media Sexploitation*, and an article 'Subliminal Seduction', states that we are inundated by subliminals every time we read a magazine, watch television, take in a movie or look at a political poster. The mind perceives faster than the eye, picking up the message that the advertiser wants to implant in your subconscious. The frightening thing is that it may be impossible to resist instructions given in this manner. Dr Key is a psychologist with a great deal of experience in communications and advertising research. Others may have discovered subliminal manipulation before Key, but his books have served to bring the matter before the public.

His books show quite graphically that phallic symbols are built into advertisements, and he says the pictures of politicians have the word sex written all over them in order to make the candidate more attractive. One such portrait of President Carter, placed under ultra violet light, was seen to be covered with the word. Ice cubes in drink ads are filled with ghoulish images which carry subliminal messages. A particular cigarette advertisement actually has the word cancer air-brushed into it, on the basis that if you smoke you are trying to kill yourself anyway. Key points out that even currency does not escape this subliminal treatment. Look at President Lincoln's beard on a $5 bill and you will see the word SEX tucked away in the strands of hair. Key says that:

> The United States may well be one of the most repressed societies on earth — purposefully educated in vast areas of reality avoidance. This is an extremely dangerous condition that could threaten both individual and national, if not world survival.

Dr Key's most recent book, *The Clam-Plate Orgy*, is another best seller in which he shows that American school children are hypnotized by the media to eat junk foods rather than a wholesome diet. Reviewers quite rightly say that his books are 'chilling' in their implications. Once you have read them you will see very clearly just how easy it is to place instructions subliminally with images, colours and juxtaposed forms, into the lower-mind body and the substance of the desire or emotional body. The daily implantation of these images reinforces their effect until they begin to circulate in the aura and take on a life of their own. When Fred Kimball reads an aura he places his own colour into the aura of the subject to enhance what is there — imagine if you will how the television is able to do this day in and day out through advertisements which subliminally play upon your passive and entranced energy fields. It is a matter worth looking into when considering the nature of auric pollution.

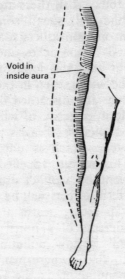

Void in inside aura

Figure 8.3 Loss of continuity of inner aura following an appendectomy (from Bagnall, The Origin and Properties of the Human Aura*)*

Drugs, whether used for recreational or medical purposes, fill the body and psyche with all manner of pollution and distorting patterns, none of which clarify our view of the world.

Osler wrote that the desire to take medicine is perhaps the greatest feature which distinguishes man from animals. In Britain alone this year the National Health Service will issue something like 28,000,000 prescriptions for mood changing drugs, which says something about the mental and emotional auras of a great many people. They do not like life as they see it through confused and clouded auras, and they have been conditioned by the media to believe that their confusion can be eliminated by chemical means. These chemical relaxants and anti-depressants are addictive and create dependence. There are more drug addicted housewives in Britain today than there are addicts on the hard drugs. The public will spend somewhere in the region of £62 million on pain killers for headaches and the relief of colds and minor aches and pains. If you consider for a moment that this level of drug ingestion is going on all over the world, even in the less developed countries where obsolete and discarded drugs are sold to the populace willy-nilly irrespective of what is wrong with them, then you have a picture of mass pollution of the human body and psyche which is unparalleled in the history of mankind. This has all happened in the last few decades since the advent of 'wonder drugs' and no one knows what the long-term effects will be. The short-term side effects are very apparent; deaths from anti-inflammatory drugs, birth defects of a horrifying magnitude. Estrogen from the Pill is now polluting public water supplies and in Puerto Rico, where many of these contraceptive pills are manufactured, the rise in cancer is high, children are being grossly deformed with young boys developing single female-shaped breasts on one side of their chests. Female children are menstruating at four years of age, and loosing their ovaries at only twelve months old due to cysts and suspected cancer. Iatrogenic, that is doctor-caused disease, is now rampant throughout the world and this is due, for the most part, to drugs. Drugs if used properly are a blessing to mankind; used indiscriminately they pollute the gross and subtle anatomy of man to the point of physical and spiritual insensibility.

At the level of the etheric body and the health aura,

there is a growing awareness of what pollutants can do. The outcry against devitalized food, white flour and white sugar is increasing. The public are aware that food additives, colourings and preservatives can inflict damage on health. Allergies are an expression of people's resistance to the life-force tainted by pollution. The resistance to mass medication through fluoridation of the public water supply is indicative of a shift in beliefs. Fluoride, incidentally, from an esoteric point of view, dulls the thinking processes and takes the sharp edge from the mind and intellect. We may wonder why such strong efforts are made by local councils to legislate it into the water supply.

While we can choose our food with care and view the media with discrimination, it is often very difficult to avoid the 'Sapper'. Sappers are people who have a unique facility for plugging into your aura and siphoning off energy, often at an alarming rate. We have all met people who leave us exhausted after being in their company for a while, and as they leave we let go of a sigh of relief. That sigh, with its drawing in and sharp expulsion of breath, actually helps to sever the link they have set up between their aura and your own. Sappers are usually people with a fairly heavy neurosis, but often it is not in evidence. They may be bordering on the morose, but more often than not they are people who move nervously and quickly. They talk fast and fix you with their eyes in order to draw energy from your aura. Inevitably they work through their solar plexus and astral body, instinctively seeking out your weak point, which is almost always your own solar plexus. Emotive subjects as a topic of conversation are the standard ploy to get you into resonance with them. The moment you empathize you are hooked, or rather they are hooked into you.

Shafica Karagulla describes in *Breakthrough to Creativity* how sappers work to draw energy from people. One technique involves the projection of a group of subtle tentacle-like streams of energy which emerge from the solar plexus of the sapper. These slip into the aura of the 'victim' and draw out energy, leaving the individual feeling drained. References to tentacle-like structures and the solar plexus are to be found elsewhere, for example Castaneda in *A Separate Reality* describes how brujo Don Genaro makes a physically impossible climb across the face of a waterfall with the aid of tentacles that emerged from the middle of his body. Not all sappers use this method, however; some use their voice and eyes, speaking quickly and closely scanning your face seeking eye to eye contact. Their eyes are often slightly bulging and held in a fixed stare. Others just sit quietly and look intently at people. Karagulla describes one such lady at a party. While everyone arrived in high spirits she was subdued. Then, taking up a comfortable position, she proceeded during the evening to stare at one party goer after another. As their energy levels dropped hers rose until she was vital and lively and they were all wondering why they felt so depleted.

Sappers are very difficult to deal with unless you immediately register their psychic approach to your aura. For the most part they are unconsciously trying to draw on your energies, but unconscious or not they are usually very persistent in their attempt. The moment they meet resistance and cannot set up the link to begin their siphoning operation, they will become agitated and use various ploys to distract your guard. A favourite one for the lady sapper is to initiate a search in her handbag for the car keys which will absolutely refuse to come to light. She clucks and complains that she can never find anything in her handbag, and may even tip the entire contents out on a suitable surface in order to distract you long enough to gain a hold on your aura. I find this a very symbolic scenario because these people rarely have the key to their own energies and feelings, and they need to feed on others. Another ploy is to make a veiled but barbed remark about you that sets your astral body into heightened activity, and in that moment you may just drop your shield long enough to get hooked. If that does not work they will activate your astral body by trying to get your sympathetic response to a situation. They play games like 'poor little me', 'victim', or 'kick me', anything to get your guard down.

The only way to deal with sappers, provided of course you are sensitive enough to register their approach, is to shut down your astral aura. You do this by holding a completely detached attitude to what they are saying; don't be sympathetic, and remain non-committal in your response. If necessary bring down an invisible shield between yourself and the sapper and mentally see it acting as a barrier to his probe. If necessary silently tell them that they cannot have your energy; if you are in their company for any length of time you may have to repeat this refusal again and again, particularly if they keep on chattering. Almost everyone knows someone who saps energy in the ways described here, and it is as well to know how to protect yourself because this kind of contact is frequently unpleasant and besides which it constitutes a form of auric pollution.

Engaging in idle gossip is a sure way to pollute your aura, particularly if the discussion is critical of others who are not present, and more especially if disease is the topic of conversation. Let us take a hypothetical case. Two ladies meet whilst out shopping, they get into conversation and the talk veers towards a neighbour they do not especially like who is presently very ill. At the physical level their sick neighbour may be several miles away; however, as the two ladies, whose auras have bonded through mutual agreement, stand and discuss some of the more unpleasant aspects of their neighbour's disease and character, an intense signal is generated in their astral and mental aura. This signal will automatically link them to the aura of the distant sick neighbour whom they are slating in no uncertain terms. At this point she will join them in a passive listening state, not physically of course, but psychically and out of linear time and space. Now we have three auras blended and linked together, each one feeding the other a blend of very potent and pathological energies. The sickness of the neighbour enters the fields of the gossiping ladies, and, while they will not contract the illness, they may wonder for days afterwards why they feel off colour. It is surprising at times how accurate our descriptions are – they are certainly going to feel off colour because their auras have picked up a potent charge of the colours of disease circulating in the neighbour's aura. When someone at a distance is talking about us, we may register the impact of that conversation especially if it is loaded with astral or emotional energy. We may say to ourselves or a companion 'Someone is talking about me, my ears are burning.' Normally this phrase is said in jest because we are too sophisticated to believe such nonsense. The Aboriginal would not be so blind, he would go aside, sit quietly and 'listen' to the distant conversation. There is an old saying that chickens come home to roost – the 'chickens' of critical and malicious gossip make a point of doing so, and they roost in the aura of the originator, distorting it and colouring it with unpleasant muddy hues of green and yellowy-browns.

It becomes evident as we study the human aura that it plays a most important role in our lives, and that we communicate and express ourselves through the aura in many ways. The colours and thought-forms circulating in it reflect out into our environment and literally colour it. We look at the world through our auras, so it is important to have an aura that is as free and clear of conflicting currents of energy and colours as possible. It is essential to allow thought-forms of bias, anger, greed, fear and resentment to die from attrition; do not resist or fight them, just let them die out by replacing them with the power of harmlessness. To be harmless in thought, word and deed throughout each day not only clears the aura more effectively than any other technique, it speeds up your inner growth as nothing else can. At the physical level we can see to it that we eat the right foods, and get the right amount of rest and recreation. We should avoid polluting our systems with smoking and excesses of alcohol; the former constricts the aura whilst the latter can expand it to the point where it loses its resilience altogether and allows obsessive entities to gain control. Possession is a very real danger when alcohol or drugs are used in excess because they open up barriers and protective layers in the aura which serve to maintain the integrity of the field. The effects of cocaine and other hard drugs are well documented; they literally unravel the energy fields of the etheric body and health aura to the point where they can no longer act as a carrier of the life-force. The effect upon the astral and mental auras is even more devastating. The term 'spaced out' as used in drug taking circles has an ominous ring to it, and in subtle terms is literally true. The junkie does become spaced out in that the natural insulation in his aura that separates it from the planetary field breaks down. When this happens his field is open to all that takes place in the planetary aura at the astral level: terrifying visions, monstrous beings and all manner of psychic violence flow into his aura and he has no control over these forces. If he keys into the higher levels of the astral plane then the input may take the form of visions of a religious and spiritual nature. Those who 'trip out' on hallucinogenic drugs may set the scene by meditating, burning incense and reading from spiritual and philosophical texts. By doing this the auras of those who are going to take the drug are programmed to resonate with the higher astral levels. If a drug is taken under poor conditions of stress and without due care then the trip is most likely to turn out to be a 'bummer' with unpleasant and frightening overtones. Irrespective of whether a drug trip turns out to be a so-called good one or a disaster, it can only serve to bring destructive and involutionary forces into the aura, thus delaying progress towards real spiritual awareness.

9

Cleansing and healing the aura

Each of us is encased in an armour which we soon, out of familiarity, cease to notice. There are only moments which penetrate it and stir the soul to sensibility.

The Way of Response — Martin Buber

Having read of the ways in which the aura can become polluted and distorted by all manner of everyday happenings, it is not surprising that we instinctively and automatically harden our aura against the environment and the various influences that fill it. At the emotional and mental levels this hardening constitutes the 'character armour' that Wilhelm Reich illustrated so clearly in his work and writings. On the physical level we are all like people living next to the railway lines: we detune ourselves to a host of impressions, and become selective in what we want to receive. Carried to extremes this shuts out impressions that are vitally important to our physical and psychological well-being, and if we are not careful this can create a narrow world that encases us like a vice. In a Rosicrucian text, 'The Brittle Aura' (in Regush, 1974), it says:

Man in his ignorance, believes he has control of himself by placing a hard exterior, first to his body, then to his mind, by appearing immovable, and third, to his soul by seeming and appearing to be unemotional and protected by a brittle aura. He then feels pride; he is in full command of himself. Nothing can reach him! Nothing can touch him! Yes — he is right, — nothing *can* touch him, nothing *can* reach him. *He is a slave to himself. He is imprisoned within himself and knows it not*. He is a sad spectacle and is ignorant of the fact.

The text goes on to say that the aura is like a protective skin or outer covering, and to a large extent it is the key to the human soul, because through the aura one reaches the soul of another. The protective instinct, largely fuelled by fears of known and unknown things, causes the aura to become brittle, rather like a silk lampshade does when it is left too close to a hot bulb. In this condition it easily breaks or tears, leaving openings through which influences can penetrate, or vital energies can leak out. Treatments with radium and X-rays burn the fluid-like forces out of the tenuous matter of the aura and similarly leave it in a brittle state, and the patient nauseous and enervated.

The Rosicrucians say that the brittle aura is one of the greatest obstacles to spiritual growth, and like a dry, cracked and brittle skin condition it needs treatment from within and from without. The cure comes from within but help from outside can be applied in the form of baths with the herb rosemary added. Rudolph Steiner strongly advocates the use of rosemary to balance out the etheric strands of the health aura. Moschus or musk is another remedy which is most helpful, and the wild oat *avena sativa* in mother tincture form boosts the radiance of the aura and raises resistance and vitality.

The human aura not only indicates the *vitality of the body*, but the vitality of the soul as well. It is an emanation of a radio-active nature and envelopes all of man's vehicles. The human aura, therefore, can be called man's *spiritual skin*, for it is sensitive to both inner and outer impacts. It can be translucent, opaque, thick, heavy, light, radiant, thin as tissue and impenetrable as the strongest steel at the same time. It can be porous as a sponge, brittle as glass, and soggy as mud. ('The Brittle Aura')

The aura is a receiver and a deflector of energies and impressions, from the most gross to those which are barely discernible. Receptivity depends on the state of the aura, which ideally should be radiant and filled with light. It is a fact that many sensitive people have difficulty in mixing in crowds or feeling comfortable at a party or meeting because they soak up so many conflicting impressions from those around them. This leaves them in a state of fatigue or feeling 'strung out' — this term may well be a clue to the quality of their aura which is too open, and far too receptive. These sensitives are often introverted by nature and many tend to pride themselves on the fact that they can only mix with other 'sensitive souls' on the same wavelength, and take it as a sign of spiritual status. In truth a person with a properly harmonized and balanced aura can mix with anyone and anywhere without coming away feeling any the worse for the encounter. The introverted sensitive is often a fearful person who suffers from anxiety and doubt, and these produce an unhealthy, uncontrolled form of auric sensitivity. Fear and anxiety open the individual up to obsessive powers, fear actually providing the door through which they can enter. The sages point out that fear and love cannot coexist in one person; where love is truly present its radiance projects an aura through which no negative or enervating forces can enter. Hence the emphasis placed upon love throughout the Mystery Teachings.

Love is the pivotal energy around which life revolves and evolves. It is not readily contacted nor easily expressed — consideration, caring, thoughtfulness, patience and understanding are keys to love, but not love itself. Love is paradoxically immediately available but highly elusive and until we learn to recognize its quality and have the ability to flood our auras with it, the need for interim techniques to cleanse and heal the aura will remain.

There are many books on psychic self-defense that outline any number of protective exercises. It is a subject that carries a large measure of glamour with it. Rather than search within for the reasons that lie at the root of their problems, people often prefer to think that they are under psychic attack, or that the forces of cosmic evil are out to deflect them from some great service to humanity that they have been guided from the inner planes to carry out. Tell someone in psychic circles that you are feeling drained of energy, and almost invariably they will tell you to put a circle of light around yourself. Now while this is a useful thing to do at times, it is fraught with dangers if carried on as an exercise, day in and day out. To put a circle around oneself in the form of visual-ized light is to encircle the aura with an impenetrable line of energy which in the fullness of time will let nothing in or out. This type of exercise has too many negative connotations to it. Firstly it is separative, the circle cutting the individual off from the rest of the world which con-tains some threatening element to their well-being. More subtly it implies that the person who is trying to protect themselves is somewhat special to have been singled out for attack. It is worth remembering that no negative forces can penetrate the aura unless it already contains the image of that negative force within it. More often than not it is the presence of some peculiarity, some bias or thought of greed that invites attack and enables the disruptive force to enter the aura.

Psychic attack is of course a reality; it can and does happen. What can be done, then, that will be constructive and provide protection that is not at the same time a prison? We can learn, I think, from the example of the magicians who drew a circle around themselves for the purpose of protection during magical work, filling it with all manner of symbols. The circle is an archetypal pattern that protects the one who stands within it. It is also a symbol of power. Once again it becomes necessary to look beyond the form of the circle and not take the process of drawing a circle around ourselves literally. The deepest form of protection comes from the ability to step in consciousness into the mandala of the soul. This of course presupposes a great deal of Self-knowledge and the ability to recognize and register the quality of energies that comprise the soul. Clearly this is not an easy task and certainly it is one that takes a long time to master. In the meantime there are a number of procedures that can be followed that will cleanse and enhance the sensitivity of the aura without creating a rigid barrier that can only distort reality, and hinder the progress of the pilgrim on his way.

One of the most interesting series of exercises to cleanse the auric fields is to be found in two books entitled *The Armour of Light* written by Olive Pixley, both of which contain a wealth of information. It is impossible to go into all of the exercises and details here, but sufficient can be given to provide a background for further study and application of these methods.

Olive Pixley began her work in 1917 when her brother passed over. A communication began between his world and hers which led in time to such a state of sensitivity on her part that she received direct visions of the rituals employed by the priests and neophytes of the Egyptian, Mithraic and Hermetic Mystery schools in their worship of the true Light. Finally she was shown the Christian Initiations and made aware that humanity had down through the ages polluted its bloodstream with fear, greed, cruelty and anxiety. It was made clear to her that the only way that the blood of humanity could be cleansed was through the sacrifice of some great entity who through complete selflessness, fearlessness and love would purify it.

Jesus of course fulfilled that role and Pixley's work revolves around the transmuting and transforming power of Light and Love. At first she kept her work very much to herself, feeling that it was a sacred and rather personal trust, but before long it became obvious that she had to share and teach what she had learned. A conflict arose within her regarding the abandonment of the exercises so that she could get back to the life of a normal young lady, but she found that she could not break away from the technique, and as soon as she decided to share what she had learned everything fell into place in her life.

Pixley emphasizes that we must be normal, practical people, with our feet on the ground but able to function efficiently in both the physical and the inner worlds, avoiding self-indulgence in either of them.

> Self-indulgence and self-pity are corroding conditions, and insulate one's receptivity. One must never be a 'duty martyr', making the recipient of a service conscious of the effort. Love is serving of need. When these daily lessons in Light become part of our physical substance, we shall find we can discern between need and demand. When it is a need, our heart will satisfy it; when merely a demand, our minds can receive the inspiration to refuse without hurt.

The text often speaks of seeing the Light, but it has to be pointed out that this 'seeing' may not be a literal fact, and those that practise the exercise and do not actually feel that they have seen anything should not be discouraged.

> Whether you actually see the Light that you will draw daily into your flesh and blood is immaterial. When you think of it, it is there, whether you register it consciously or not, and you are bound to feel different. Feeling and seeing in Light seem often identical. The feeling is so vivid, it corresponds to sight.

The general purpose of the exercises, Pixley points out, is the complete reconstruction of the self, including the actual substance of the physical body. Although this may sound like a rather extravagant claim it is well within the realms of possibility. The transformative power of the inner Light can be remarkable — witness for example the instantaneous cure of Brugh Joy's potentially terminal illness which was accompanied by a brilliant flash of light, and the inspired writing of Mary Fullerson in her two books, *By a New and Living Way* and *The Form of the Fourth*. The procedures she followed transformed her blood picture to the point where it showed clearly in clinical tests that the whole cell structure had changed for the better.

In all of the exercises outlined by Olive Pixley she stresses that the breath is the carrier of sound and light forces. The light is visualized as a force and not merely seen as a symbol. The technique starts off by using the visualized conscious breathing to create a track between God the Father, Christ the mediating principle between Spirit and matter, and the human being who is to receive the transforming power of the Light. Pixley insists that each exercise must be followed in a particular order, beginning with what she calls the Ritual of Light, and that it is important to master each exercise in turn before even reading about the next one. This being the case I propose only to give the first exercise; for those who wish to go into these techniques further, her books must be studied.

When you wake in the morning lie relaxed in every joint, and especially in the head. Then think a radiant Figure of Light at your feet, with the soles of your feet touching the soles of this Figure. This contact with the feet is the necessary earth for Divine power to spark through the body. Once you have earthed your Figure of Light, it is there as a Light to your path for

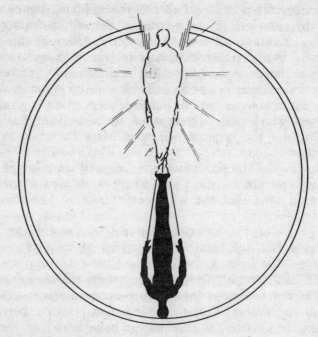

Figure 9.1 Ritual of Light

the rest of the day. The next second, send your vision soaring upwards until you see above you an Infinite Point of Light, which is God. That point is the station from which inspiration and revelation can be flashed into your mind throughout the day, whenever you choose to re-focus your mind upon it. Having now your earth and your mental focussing point, instantaneously think a flashing circle from the right of your head round the Head of the Figure of Light back to your own head, thus completing the circle. The radiant image of Christ sanctifies your feet for the day's activity, and your mind is made capable of receiving inspiration. Whether it does so or not depends on you.

This ritual must be a daily renewal of strength, our

daily Bread of Life. Don't let the mind wander, or
dwell lingeringly; let it flash and then finish. This
trains our minds to spark, for one cannot meditate
on or contemplate a flash of lightening. One must
not linger on any part of the Technique in Light: it
is a quickening process in every sense of the word,
and should be done so quickly that even the busiest
people can spare a flashing moment every morning
for the reception of their daily Bread.

Having done this exercise, lie completely relaxed, the
palms of your hands upward by your sides and the soles
of your feet in contact with the Figure of Light. See the
Infinite Point of Radiance above you, and as you do so,
inhale gently and deeply and visualize the breath going
down the outside of the body from the level of the solar
plexus to your feet. As you exhale visualize the breath
going from the solar plexus straight to the Infinite Point
above you. Repeat this process at least six times following the Ritual of Light. The exercise should always be
done first thing in the morning, but it can be repeated
during the day if you are stressed, in order to re-establish
equilibrium.

Another very potent exercise for cleansing the various
layers of the aura and connecting with the inner Light
is one that I devised for use in healing workshops, which
I call Curtains of Light. In a workshop situation the
process of guided imagery is employed but it is a simple
matter to take oneself through the various phases of the
exercise.

Assume a relaxed and comfortable position, close your
eyes and regulate your breathing. Visualize three circular
curtains of light flowing downwards and disappearing into
the floor. The outer curtain is a sparkling golden-yellow,
the next curtain inwards is a beautiful rose pink, and the
third a clear electric-blue. In the centre of these three
curtains of light is a vibrant orb of radiant white, hovering

above the floor.

See yourself in profile standing in front of the curtain of golden-yellow light, visualize its flowing downward movement. Silently sound the aum and step forward through the curtain. Visualize the light flowing right through your etheric and physical body, and see the solidity of your form give way to a body of golden light, and the dross and toxins that were in the etheric dropping away on the outside of the curtain and dissolving.

Now you are facing the curtain of rose pink energies which symbolize your astral or emotional body. Once again silently sound the aum and step forward through the curtain. Its energies will sweep through your emotional body like water, cleansing the fears, anxieties and stresses from it. See them drop away as you pass through the curtain and dissolve into nothing.

You now face the electric-blue curtain of the mental body. Silently repeat the aum and step forward, seeing any negative thought patterns and beliefs drop away behind you. As you carry out each phase of this visualization you can actually feel the weight of acquired negative patterns drop away.

Before you now is the floating orb of radiant white light — the transpersonal self or the Christ within. It brings with it a deep sense of reverence, of enfolding peace and love. Your cares have vanished, for in this area of consciousness stress and pain are unknown. Jesus said, 'Come unto me, all of you who are heavy laden and I will give you rest.' You can now touch upon the energy of his words.

Stand before the Light with your head bowed, or if you feel moved to kneel in reverence then do so. Absorb the Light into your cleansed aura, see it expand into a beautiful radiance of colours, filled with Love. Nothing negative can penetrate it now. In your own time turn and face outwards towards the world of form, and step through each curtain of light in turn adding an extra radiance to them, until you step beyond the golden-yellow curtain of the etheric level. Stand for a moment, recall the orb of Light at the centre of your being and raise your arms up and spread them outwards. As you do so, sound the aum silently and breathe out a blessing upon your immediate environment and then on and outwards to the world and humanity at large. Always give of the Light you have contacted, because in this giving you receive.

This exercise when carried out regularly has a remarkable effect upon the aura. The sounding of the holy word aum, vibrating between the palate and the pineal gland, thrills through the attenuated substance of the etheric, astral and mental bodies, shaking out the coarse atoms and discharging them from the aura. Visualizing the appropriate colour of each body enhances this effect and the result is a heightening of consciousness and a deep and thorough cleansing of the auric layers associated with each body. It has the advantage that no defensive barriers are constructed against inimical forces, nor are they given any attention. The power of Light and Love is utilized to produce a vital field which simply does not attract negative energies. Through the heart, the Love of God is shed abroad. There is no greater protection.

Colour has always been considered one of the most effective modalities for treating the aura and enjoyed great popularity in the earlier decades of this century, both here and abroad. Dr Edwin Babbitt earned fame as a colour therapist, and in the 1930s Dinshah P. Ghadiali, also practising colour therapy in the United States, made a deep study of the subject. Unfortunately he had a weakness for attacking the Establishment, and they finally turned nasty and put all of his equipment to the sledge hammer and banned him from practising. On this side of the Atlantic, Dr E.C. Iredell, who was surgeon-emeritus of the actino-therapeutic department of Guy's

Hospital, London, was busily treating cancer patients with a colour instrument he called a Focal Machine. Despite the fact that every patient he dealt with had been operated on and exposed to heavy doses of X-rays and the like, he got remarkably encouraging results. Patients were relieved of pain, their nausea disappeared and they felt better in themselves.

Iredell wrote a book on his work, entitled *Colour and Cancer*, which has long been out of print. He reports at length on the sensations occurring in patients' bodies during exposure to colour treatments. He writes:

> It may be of interest here to give some rough idea of the effects of the colours used as described by some patients who were sufficiently sensitive to feel them. The colour most generally used was bright green. The sensation it produced was generally described as cool and pleasant, but not very smooth. It was soothing when the patient was restless. It was also the colour with which it was found advisable to begin and end all treatments, as the effects of the other colours were intensified if an application of green was given after they had been used.
>
> A deep royal blue generally followed the use of green, but it was liable to produce depression if given for more than a short time.

Iredell reports that too much yellow increased pain. Violet, which he used after yellow, produced a smoother and finer feeling then green, but it had to be used in conjunction with other colours when its effects then became quite striking. Reds and oranges were seldom used, but orange proved to be useful as a stimulant and was helpful in cases of indigestion. One of the most interesting experiences that many of Iredell's patients consistently reported was that they felt as though water was running down their bodies during colour treatment. This feeling was so strong that they would reach for a handkerchief to wipe the wet away only to find themselves quite dry. It seems evident that these patients were experiencing the loosening up to the flow of energies through their auras as the colours applied to the body began to have a healing effect. Iredell experimented with all manner of ideas, pulsing the colour to synchronize with breathing and pulse rates, and placing patients in circular enclosures of dull black material to enhance the effects of the colour.

While Iredell's approach required expensive equipment, it is possible to employ colour for therapeutic purposes in other ways. Colour breathing, for example, is one method which anyone can learn to use in order to heal or simply refresh themselves. S.G. Ouseley wrote a booklet on the subject of colour healing under the title *The Power of the Rays*, in which he describes a variety of ways to use colour, amongst them colour breathing and the colour pass.

To carry out colour breathing exercises sit comfortably in a chair, relax and close your eyes. Determine which colour you require, remembering that yellow is a tonic for the nervous system, reds and oranges increase vitality, blues induce calmness and greens soothe and energize. You can use several colours during one treatment if you wish. Having determined the correct colour, breathe deeply and steadily in for the count of six and visualize yourself gathering the colour you want on the breath. Hold for a count of three and then breathe out to the count of six. As you do so, see the colour you have selected flood throughout your aura. Just as the colours can be changed so can the count: 6-3-6 is a useful pattern but 8-4-8 can be used to good effect, or in fact any particular combination you find best as you experiment with this method of self-healing.

The colour pass is used by the healer to treat a patient, who should sit comfortably in a chair, relaxed and eyes closed. The healer stands in front of the patient and brings to mind the colour he wishes to transmit to the patient, and through concentration he builds up a charge of this colour in his aura. At the same time an affirmation of intent can be made silently by the healer, such as: 'I will restore the vitality of this patient through the use of the colour orange.' Hands clenched, the healer raises them above the head of the patient and then brings them down in a sweeping movement past the forehead, face, throat, chest and on downwards until the whole body has been traversed. The colour pass should take about thirty seconds to complete and should be repeated for five minutes or so. At the end of each pass the hands should be flicked to get rid of any effluvia picked up from the patient's aura. This procedure can be applied to patients at a distance, and all the healer has to do is visualize the patient sitting on a chair and himself going through the same movements. This can prove to be a remarkably effective method of distant treatment, provided you keep in mind that at the level that mental treatment is carried out, there is no time or space. Patient and healer are together just as if they were together at the physical level.

In 1979 Dolores Krieger's book *The Therapeutic Touch* was published. She outlined a whole series of hand to body contact movements which were designed to bring harmony to the energy fields of the body, relieve pain and restore health. Krieger, a Ph.D., an R.N. and professor of nursing at New York University, took the techniques used by healers for centuries and gave them an aura of respectability by calling them therapeutic touch. She says that the book developed out of nine years of research on healing, six years of clinical application of the techniques, and five years of teaching this ancient method of healing in its modern guise. By 1979 she had taught the techniques of therapeutic touch to 350 professional nurses and over 4,000 health care professionals in universities throughout Canada and the United States.

The techniques are varied and simple and highly effective once you have grasped the principles of applying them. It is not my intention to go into details here, but simply to outline one particular technique which has an immediate and clearly registered effect upon the aura. This technique is called 'unruffling' and is carried out with the patient lying in a prone position with his hands at his sides. The healer then places both his hands over the top of the patient's head, just lightly touching the hair. Spreading the hands apart they should run lightly down the length of the body to the feet. This move should be repeated several times, then switched from the head to the finger tips of the patient. These same moves can be carried out with the patient lying supine so that the front of the body is also treated. This form of treatment seems to take out all of the kinks and distortions from the aura, and the beneficial effects can be felt immediately. By adding colour visualization to the movements the depth of healing can be enhanced.

These then are some of the visualization exercises and healing techniques which will help to restore harmony and integrity to the aura. Applied with care and common sense they can only prove beneficial. There are obviously many other approaches equally valid, but it is best to select those which appeal to you most and practise them until you reach a level of proficiency and sensitivity wherein you are able to effectively cleanse your aura and maintain the integrity of each layer on a daily basis, thus keeping at bay those forces and influences that are deleterious to health.

10

The influence of gems

The well-formed image of a lion, if engraved on a garnet,
will protect and preserve honors and health, cures the wearer
of all diseases, brings him honors, and guards him from all
perils in travelling.

Book of Wings — Ragiel

Precious and semi-precious stones have long been recognized as potent carriers of healing and protective influences. This recognition spans the centuries and is found in all societies, from the most primitive tribal groups to the civilizations of Ancient Egypt and Greece. Man has an innate love of gem stones that arises from their resonance with the mineral strata of his own being. They are a part of his being — we are made from the substance of the stars and connected with the universe through the energy frequencies of the mineral world. Little wonder that, when these minerals organize themselves into specific groupings to produce precious stones, we set great store by their influences upon our health and well-being.

Gems were used by prehistoric man, no doubt to give him protection and make him 'invisible' to the inner eye of predators. Crystals have been held in high esteem for well over forty thousand years, and used as power objects or for purposes of divination. During his initiation the Aboriginal shaman has many crystals placed inside his body by magical means, and one is 'rubbed' into his forehead to give him the power of far-seeing through the third eye. The Pharaohs, the Aztecs and the Incas, the mandarins of China and the seers and sages of India knew the esoteric lore of gems as power objects. The ancient astrologers believed that gems possessed specific planetary influences, and the natal gems were used to ward off evil and malefic planetary energies. In the 1600s physicians believed that benefic influences were placed in precious stones by the grace of God, to guard men from danger and to attract wealth and position. Many were the powers ascribed to gems in those days: apart from making you rich they were said to preserve men from thunder and lightning, plagues and diseases of all kinds, to divine the future, ward off insomnia, hinder laziness and witchcraft, keep men chaste and make them invisible.

There may be grounds to question such powers ascribed to gems by physicians three hundred years ago, but there is interesting evidence from the early 1800s when experiments were run with a sensitive, one Frederike Hauffe (b.1801), known as the 'Seeress of Prevorst' and said to have extraordinary powers of clairvoyance. To determine the effects of various stones and gems upon her, a whole range were laid out and she touched them each in turn with unusual results, many of them quite dramatic. Granite or flint had no effect, whereas fluorspar produced a sour taste in her mouth, relaxed muscles and gave her diarrhoea. Sapphire and Iceland spar produced a somnambulant state, while sulphate of barium did quite the opposite creating a warmth in her body and muscular stimulation. The sulphate of barium had an added bonus in that it made her laugh and feel as though she could fly through the air. Rock crystal had the power to bring her out of trance, but if left on her stomach it stiffened all of her muscles and threw her into an epileptic state, her muscles becoming so rigid that they resisted all efforts to bring about movements in her joints. Oxide of iron literally paralysed her on the spot and produced a sensation of inner chill. Unfortunately for the seeress diamonds had a similar effect, so did not turn out, as popularly supposed, to be her best friend. Magnetite caused sensations of heaviness and convulsions of the limbs. Ruby produced a sensation of coldness in the tongue and virtually paralysed her vocal chords, and caused violent shivers to run through her body.

This illustration of the effects certain stones and minerals can have on a sensitive points out that we should take care in our selection of stones or gems for personal adornment. Many years ago a friend of mine decided to wear an authentic Maori tiki made from green soapstone. He wore it around his neck and against his body. Within a few days he began to experience uncomfortable chest pains, but did not connect them with the tiki. Finally he made an appointment with his doctor about the persistent pains. Not wishing to appear rather odd or unconventional in front of his surburban doctor, he removed the tiki, and as he lifted it over his head the pain immediately cleared from his chest. Having lived in New Zealand and known that the tiki was an amulet to be worn by pregnant women, he realized what a mistake he had made. It went back in a drawer where it had lain for years, and he has not worn it since.

Just as the colour of the clothes we wear can be seen as a reflection of auric colours, so gems and semi-precious stones are a similar indication of the colours and patterns of the aura. In some instances they may be used to enhance colours already present, or, if there is a lack, the stone will add colour and lustre to the aura, provided of course it is suitable for the individual concerned. Giacinto Gimma, who lived in Naples during the 1700s, wrote several volumes on the significance of the colours of precious stones, gathering together a great deal of information on the subject, linking colours, stones, animals and a whole host of other related factors from astrology to the days of the week.

Gimma wrote that yellow worn by a man denoted secrecy, by a woman, generosity. It was the symbol of the sun and Sunday, the zodiacal sign of Leo, and naturally the animal connected with yellow was the lion. The precious stone was yellow jacinth or chrysolite. Garments of yellow were a sign of grandeur and nobility.

Green indicated the decline of friendship, transitory hope and joyousness in men, and unfounded ambition, change and childish delight in women. Mercury and Wednesday were its planet and day, while the sly fox was the associated animal. The emerald represented youth and five was the magic number expressing it.

Red garments worn by a man indicated nobility, lordship, command and vengeance; on a woman, obstinacy, haughtiness and pride. It was the colour of Mars and Tuesday, its animal the lynx and precious stone the ruby.

Blue worn by a man symbolized the height of wisdom; on a woman, vigilance, love, politeness and jealousy. Blue was the colour ascribed to Venus and Friday. The goat and the sapphire were the designated animal and precious stone, six the magical number.

Violet worn by a man was said to denote industry, seriousness, gravity and sober judgement; on a woman, high thoughts and religious love. Like blue, the sapphire represented violet. Its planet and day were Jupiter and Thursday, its animal the bull and magic number three.

White signified for men religion, integrity and friendship. Ermine was the animal, the magic number seven. White was associated with the moon and Monday, and represented by the pearl.

So widespread was the use of precious and semi-precious stones in even the greatest of our civilizations, it is hard to dismiss the many claims for them. Much of what the ancients had to say about the healing and protective qualities of stones is readily discounted by modern man as superstition based on ignorance and fear. And yet many persist in wearing stones, gems and even metals to ward off illness. Witness the common copper bangle seen on men and women alike today, worn to ward off arthritis and rheumatism. In a moment we will consider the effects attributed to various gem stones, but before doing this I want to go back to the work on the aura done by Dr Guyon Richards and mentioned in chapter 7.

Richards, as you may recall, in the course of his medical research on the aura found that it consisted of various layers, or shells as he called them. This of course was common knowledge to clairvoyants; but Richards went further in that he discovered that minerals were what he termed one-ring biomorphs, vegetables were two-ring biomorphs, insects and reptiles were three-ring biomorphs, mammals and birds were three- and four-ring biomorphs, and man was a four- and five-ring biomorph.

It struck me as more than common coincidence that the Chinese mandarins used a five-tiered hierarchy of rank determined by religious or ceremonial considerations, and that each rank was designated by certain stones. Rank in a mandarin can only mean his level of spiritual unfoldment, and I cannot help wondering if the five ranks symbolize the perfection of each of the five layers or biomorphic rings of the aura. In *The Curious Lore of Precious Stones*, author George Kunz lists the stones symbolizing each rank and notes that red stones are given preference. Red stones as we have seen indicate nobility and lordship, the natural status of a mandarin. Red is also the symbolic colour of life, denoting strength, vigour and capability.

Kunz lists the ranks of the mandarins and their stones as follows:

Red or pink tourmaline, ruby (and rubellite)	1st rank
Coral or an inferior red stone (garnet)	2nd rank
Blue stone (beryl or lapis lazuli)	3rd rank

Rock crystal   4th rank
Other white stones   5th rank

Each colour and type of stone symbolizes each band or
ring of the aura, the red indicating the highest inner
unfoldment, the colour of the Father or Will aspect of
deity, the blue the Son aspect, and the crystal and white
stones the Mother aspect. Whatever their meaning it
would seem that there is quite possibly a connection
between the five bands of the aura and the ranks of the
mandarins.

Stones have been used for therapeutic purposes for
many thousands of years. Speculation says that Indian
shamans and physicians made such extensive use of gems
that the sheer volume of their work moved it westwards
toward Europe to become a therapeutic modality here.
Kunz points out however that the Ebers Papyrus from
Egypt recommends the use of lapis lazuli as an ingredient
for eye salve and hematite for checking haemorrhages,
so in reality the origins of gems as medicine are shrouded
in the mists of time, and no one can be sure when their
use was initiated.

Gems are employed therapeutically in a number of
ways. They may be worn for the direct influence they
have upon the energy fields of the wearer, and this is or
was one of the most common methods employed. In
India the ayurvedic physicians burned and ground them
into powder in order to make medicines. More recently
they have been immersed in phials of alcohol and stored
in complete darkness until the fluid absorbed the vibratory frequencies of the gems; the liquid is then given in
drop form for various diseases. On the subject of pulver-
izing gems there is an interesting account written by
Olaus Borrichius around 1757 and now in the Collection
Académique, Paris. It reads:

> When precious stones are to be used in medicine, they
> must be pulverized until they are reduced to a powder

so fine that it will not grate under the teeth, or, in the words of Galen, this powder must be as impalpable 'as that which is blown into the eyes.' Since this trituration is not usually operated with sufficient care by the apothecaries, I begged a medical student, who was lodging with me, to pass an entire month in grinding some of these stones. I gave him emeralds, jacinths, sapphires, rubies, and pearls, an ounce of each kind. As these stones were rough and whole, he first crushed them a little in a well-polished iron mortar, using a pestle of the same metal; afterwards he employed a pestle and mortar of glass, devoting several hours each day to this work. At the end of about three weeks, his room, which was rather large, became redolent with a perfume, agreeable both from its variety and sweetness. This odor, which much resembled that of March violets, lingered in the room for more than three days. There was nothing in the room to produce it, so that it certainly proceeded from the powder of precious stones. (Kunz, *The Curious Law of Precious Stones*)

Let us look then at some of the more commonly used precious and semi-precious stones, and list their uses according to the authorities of centuries gone by.

EMERALD

This gem has been employed as an antidote for poisons, poisoned wounds and demoniacal possession. It is said to rest and relieve the eye. An emerald worn against the abdomen was used as a cure for dysentery. It checked haemorrhages, diminished the secretion of bile and was considered a good laxative. It conferred inner-sight and revealed truth.

RUBY

Indian physicians found it a useful remedy for flatulency and bilious attacks. It shielded the wearer from adverse fortune in the midst of his enemies, and gave protection in battle.

DIAMOND

Like the emerald its special virtue was its capacity to act as an antidote to poisons. It was said to afford protection from pestilence and the plague, and cured insanity. By wearing a diamond in contact with the skin nightmares and terrible dreams can be warded off. The diamond brings victory, strength, fortitude and courage. It wards off the evil eye and contributes to personal safety.

SAPPHIRE

The sapphire was used to clear impurities from the eyes, and treat plague boils. It preserved the wearer from envy and was thought to attract divine favour. Some physicians ranked it with the emerald as an antidote to poison.

JADE

A favourite of the Chinese although not found in that country, it was used to treat stony formations such as calculi in the kidneys. When reduced to the size of rice grains it strengthened the lungs, the heart and the vocal organs. If gold and silver were added to jade powder it was thought to prolong life. A mixture of jade, dew and rice boiled in a copper pot and filtered produced the 'divine liquor of jade' which hardened bones, calmed the mind, purified the blood and made muscles strong and supple. Even the great physician Galen wrote of its efficacy as a treatment for stomach ailments when held against the body.

There are many other stones, of course, and each has its curative and protective properties. It is impossible within the context of this book to consider them all, but if we become aware that the wearing of stones and gems brings influences into our aura, and in many instances enhances its power and colour, then we should take care to select gems and stones that are appropriate to the needs of our own fields. Indiscriminate selection may well lead to the introduction of imbalances into our auras, something we can ill afford in this hectic modern world.

While the seers and physicians of the past were aware of the importance of the aura, and the protection afforded by gems and various amulets and talismanic forms, we, for the most part, have lost this awareness and knowledge. However there is evidence to suggest that the ancient practices are re-emerging in modern form, and it is predictable that there will be a resurgence of awareness regarding the importance of the aura and its protection from debilitating influences.

In California, chemical engineer Dr George Yao has developed a device called Pulsor. This is described as a modern solid state electronic microcrystal composite transceiver with ultra-wide wavebands which corrects and amplifies the body's natural aura and polarity. These microcrystal transceivers are set in attractive pendants of agate, amethyst, jasper, jade and a variety of other stones and abalone mother-of-pearl to be worn on the body. They also come in the form of rings and belt buckles. Dr Yao claims that the Pulsor creates a protective force-field around the body which removes the charge from electrons and converts them into nutrinos which have no further effect on the biophysical energy systems of the body. He points out, as radiesthetists (dowsers) have been pointing out for decades now, that telephone wiring, water and gas pipes, television radiation and electrical circuits in the home can upset the natural polarity of our energy fields, resulting in physiological imbalances that give rise to tension, anxiety and apprehension. They also lay us open to invasive forces, bacterial infections and quite probably psychic influences not compatible with health. The Pulsor device is said to offset these disturbing influences by inducing positive currents of energy into the aura, thus producing a protective shield around the wearer.

While it is obvious that the best way to maintain a healthy aura is to be focused on the higher levels of consciousness, and to balance this vertical focus with the practical horizontal expression of physical plane awareness, man has always sought to augment his strength and harmony with some form of exterior device, whether it be a necklace or bracelet of semi-precious stones, a talismanic pattern, a ring of precious metal, or the modern Pulsor. Provided we do not lose sight of the fact that our real power lies within, then these devices can be seen as useful adjuncts in the maintenance of balance in our auric fields.

11

A radiance of light and love and power

The mystic has the sensory perception of this irradiation of lights proceeding from the whole of his person.

Najm Kobrā

The themes of light and love and power are to be found flowing throughout the mystical and spiritual writings of the East and West. Their capacity to transform a mere human being into a superhuman state of consciousness is a fundamental tenet of all true teachings. It is said that when the Buddha reached enlightenment under the bodhi tree, his aura flared out in a spontaneous gesture of blessing, encompassing the earth and every living creature with the light of his understanding. In that instant he became the light of the world.

In the Bible we read that as Jesus underwent the initiation of Transfiguration, he became so radiant with light that Peter, James and John, who symbolize the physical, astral and mental bodies (the low-self), could not gaze upon him. He took them to the mountain or place of the high-self, and there, Matthew relates, 'Was transfigured before them: and his face did shine as the sun [soul], and his raiment [aura] was white as the light.' The Sufi mystic Najm Kobrā describes this outpouring of celestial love and union in similar words but with far more detail:

> When the circle of the face has become pure, it effuses
> lights as a spring pours forth its water, so that the
> mystic has a sensory perception that these lights are
> gushing forth to irradiate his face. This outpouring
> takes place between the two eyes and between the
> eyebrows. Finally it spreads to cover the whole face.
> At that moment, before you, before your face, there
> is another Face also of light, irradiating lights; while
> behind its diaphanous veil a *sun* becomes visible, seem-
> ingly animated by a movement to and fro. In reality
> this Face is your own face and this sun is the sun of
> the Spirit that goes to and fro in your body. Next
> the whole of your person is immersed in purity, and
> suddenly you are gazing at a person of light who is
> also irradiating lights.

Kobrā goes on to describe how the light of transformation,
having emerged from the eyes, then suffuses the face,
chest and then the entire body in a blinding radiance.
This radiance fills the aura with miraculous powers that
heal and en-lighten. In The Acts of the Apostles we read:
'Insomuch that they brought forth the sick into the
streets, and laid them on beds and couches, that at the
least the shadow of Peter passing by might overshadow
some of them.' When Peter passed by, his shadow or
aura healed the sick. This state of radiance emerges from
anyone who has made the transition from a state of
darkness or spiritual ignorance to the realms of consciousness that are described by the term light. The 91st Psalm
begins: 'He that dwelleth in the secret place of the most
High shall abide under the shadow of the Almighty.'
The realm of Light is the place of the most High, and
to penetrate this high-energy frontier we have to be
able to vibrate in synchronicity with Its frequency. Our
mental, emotional and physical bodies must be free and
clear of fear, anxiety, prejudices, anger, pride and greed,

for these act like points of friction when the high frequency energies of the soul strikes them. The resultant irritation and inflammation that is set up fills the aura with darkness that gives rise to physical and psychological pathology. The oldest known prayer in the world reflects clearly the two fundamental divisions of consciousness. It goes: 'Lord, lead us from darkness to light, from the unreal to the real, from death to immortality.' This is a remarkable statement when you consider its implications. First it tells us that we live in an unreal world of darkness and death — the valley of the shadow (aura) of death. But beyond this dark world lies a world that is real, and this world is a world of light that bestows immortality. The Sufis speak of the Earth of Light, the *Terra Lucida*, and in all mystical teachings there are detailed descriptions of the geography of these higher realms of consciousness. Jesus said: 'I am from above, you are from below', thus clarifying our position. We are admonished: 'Be in the world but not of it', which carries a clear enough meaning and message to those who have ears to listen. Jesus says: 'In the world ye shall have tribulation: but be of good cheer; I have overcome the world.' It becomes eventually a matter of focus: our everyday world reaches out greedily for our attention, we take in and experience all it has to offer — riches, happiness, poverty, pain, sorrow and suffering — until we have had a surfeit of them all; then like the Prodigal Son we begin our journey back to the world from which we emerged aeons ago to experience life on the lower planes of darkness and death. The mystics down through the ages have illustrated the way out of illusion and how to over-come death. They have taught power over the flesh and insisted on the reality of eternal life. We have been too busy to pay much attention until the going gets rougher and rougher; then we turn for home, driven by the urge to reunite with our Source. Fortunately the promise has been given that we too can overcome the world. As our focus of awareness moves to spiritual matters, haltingly at first and then with reassured persistence, it manifests as the vertical aspect of the cross. In some experiences we concentrate on the vertical to the exclusion of the horizontal bar of physical plane life; in other experiences we reverse this focus until we eventually become centred where the vertical and horizontal lines of energy cross each other. To be able to stand at this point of consciousness presupposes that we have cleansed our auras of deleterious and coarse matter so that the inner light can shine forth. The inner alchemy has transformed the sand of the lower-self first into glass, then crystal. The crystal is then shaped into a lens with the power to burn out all the dross from the bodies of the lower-self. This lense is the third eye through which the light of the soul pours its cleansing energies, and on a higher turn of the spiral the soul itself becomes the 'third eye' of the Spirit who brings the process of purification to its climax at the Crucifixion.

Najm Kobrā wrote of the light pouring out of the space between the eyebrows (traditionally the location of the third eye), and we find the same theme in St. Luke: 'The light of the body is the eye: therefore when thine eye is single, thy whole body is also full of light; but when *thine eye* is evil, thy body also *is* full of darkness.' Luke makes an important distinction here between the single or third eye, and *thine eye*, the eye of the lower-self. The former when fully active distributes the light of the soul, the latter can only perceive darkness or the world of the unreal.

The third eye forms when the energy fields of the pituitary and pineal glands in the head expand to the point where they overlap. The overlapping of these two circles of energy creates the lense through which the soul can finally view the lower worlds without distortion. The inner man no longer 'sees through a glass darkly' but through a finely ground and polished lense. The metaphors of glass, crystal and diamond are highly accurate in their descriptions of these aspects of the subtle anatomy. In Islamic teachings as in Vajrayana Buddhism the 'Diamond Body' is a reality produced by spiritual alchemy when the earth of our being is transformed by the Spirit: 'And diamond, freed from crystal, freed from glass, freed from stone, correspond to the believer's bodies in this absolute Paradise.' (Corbin, *The Man of Light in Iranian Sufism*)

Purity and harmlessness in thought, word and deed produce clarity, and clarity enables the inner light to express itself through the aura. In 1967 a book entitled *The Shining Stranger* was published in the United States. The author used a pen name, Preston Harold. No one knows who or what the author was, only that he is deceased and that he held a firm belief that truth, when published, made its own way into people's hearts and minds. The sub-title of the book reads: 'An unorthodox interpretation of Jesus and his Mission.' It is certainly that, because throughout its pages Preston Harold calls upon the then recent discoveries of science to serve as a basis from which to explore the life and works of Jesus. There are many references to light both with respect to Jesus and to science. Harold writes:

But as important as the second law of thermodynamics is to scientists, the study of energy, of light, is of first importance. Jesus appears to have seen that the secret of the universe must rest in *light*, primordial energy, and that in the creation of light rests the secret of creation itself. If He realized the nature of it, He must tell its story in large drama because prime energy, or elementary particle, cannot be identified and is not an individual. In making Himself a symbol of light in order to reveal its nature, and in being a symbol of saving grace in man, He took care to insure that someday men would realize His revelation was of universal truth. This is to say, He did not forget to enfold in the being of all humankind the primordial energy of God that He represented, and also to enfold in all humankind what appears to be the saving grace of life, for to the multitudes before Him, Jesus said: 'Ye are the light of the world. A city that is set on a hill cannot be hid', and: 'Let your light so shine before men, that they may see your good works, and glorify your Father which is in heaven.'

The city in most spiritual texts refers to the lower-self or personality of man. Filled with light as it would be, placed on the hill or mountain top of the soul, it cannot be hid, and is there for all to see. The good works do not refer to outer physical activities, no matter how beneficial they may be, but to the inner works of alchemy that have transformed the darkness of the stone to diamond-like clarity.

Bearing in mind the metaphor of the city and our subtle bodies, cast your eyes upon the state that our modern cities are in, the urban decay, the dirt and the constant interplay of destructive forces that takes place in them daily, and you will begin to see their auras. Look into the atmosphere over any major city and see the pollution that hangs like a pall of death over them and you will begin to observe the aura man is creating in his greed and ignorance of natural laws. In *Earth's Aura*, Louise Young writes:

Every life form has an aura characteristic of its personality; a breath, a scent, and a flow of energy emanate from it. This luminous cloud may be fragrant and radiant, or sour and dull, depending upon the inner life of the organism. A little perfume or deodorant does not improve an aura for long. Something fundamental must happen before it takes on a more vibrant and pleasing aspect.

She concludes:

Man's aura is becoming darker and more bitter year by year.

When Louise Young writes of man's aura she is referring to the aura of pollution he has thrown up around the planet earth. Her book is timely in that man is becoming aware of the aura in its many forms. He is slowly learning too that the earth is a living being whose aura we live within, and could not survive without. If it becomes too polluted it may convulse in one last ditch effort to cleanse itself, possibly in such a conflagration the human aura would receive a healing as well.

As Louise Young says, 'A little perfume or deodorant does not improve the aura for long.' Cosmetic games like 'greening' or 'blueing' up your aura on weekend workshops pale into insignificance when one realizes the seriousness and profound importance of a clear, clean aura. To purify, and to bring lasting clarity to the aura, means nothing less than total self-transformation, and that is a task that cannot be ignored, nor undertaken lightly. But it is a fundamental one that faces each of us at an individual level, and in the context of humanity as a whole.

It is said that, to those great souls who watch over humanity from the higher realms of consciousness, each human being appears as a tiny unit of light. These lights, some bright, some barely flickering, are spread over the face of this globe. In some areas there are concentrations of them, and their effect is to thin out the fogs and miasmas of fear and illusion that swirl around the subtle aura of earth. If this is so, then it is clearly an act of service to humanity if you begin the daily process of methodically filling your aura with light, and gently radiating it out upon the world in a silent blessing — seeking nothing in return and receiving everything.

THE GREAT INVOCATION

> From the point of Light within the Mind of God
> Let light stream forth into the minds of men.
> Let Light descend on Earth.

From the point of Love within the Heart of God
Let love stream forth into the hearts of men.
May Christ return to Earth.

From the centre where the Will of God is known
Let purpose guide the little wills of men —
The purpose which the Masters know and serve.

From the centre which we call the race of Men
Let the Plan of Love and Light work out
And may it seal the door where evil dwells.

Let Light and Love and Power restore the
                      Plan on Earth.

Bibliography

The Language of ESP in Action is directly available from Fred
Kimball, P.O. Box 354, Idyelwild, California 92349, USA. $12
including postage. *The Form of the Fourth* and *By a New and Living
Way* by Mary Fullerson are available from Metascience Publications,
P.O. Box 747, Franklin, North Carolina 28734, USA.

Babbitt, E., *The Principles of Light and Color*, New York, University Books Inc., 1967.

Bagnall, O., *The Origin and Properties of the Human Aura*, York Beach, Samuel Weiser Inc., 1975.

Bailey, A., *Esoteric Psychology*, vols I & II, London, Lucis Press, 1942.

Bailey, A., *Letters on Occult Meditation*, New York, Lucis Publishing Co., 1948.

Becker, R. and Marino, A., *Electromagnetism and Life*, Albany, State University of New York, 1982.

Bentine, M., *A Door Marked Summer*, London, Granada, 1981.

Berndt, R.M., 'Wuradjeri Magic and "Clever Men"', *Oceania*.

Besant, A. and Leadbeater, C.W., *Thought-Forms*, Adyar, Theosophical Publishing House, 1905.

Buber, M., *The Way of Response*, New York, Schocken Books, 1966.

Castaneda, C., *A Separate Reality*, London, Bodley Head, 1971.

Castaneda, C., *Journey to Ixtlan*, New York, Simon & Schuster, 1972.

Cayce, E., *Auras*, Virginia Beach, A.R.E. Press, 1945.

Corbin, H., *Spiritual Body and Celestial Earth*, Princeton, Bollingen Series XCI:Z, Princeton University Press, 1977.

Corbin, H., *The Man of Light in Iranian Sufism*, Boulder, London, Shambhala, 1978.

Davies, P., *God and the New Physics*, London, Toronto & Melbourne, J.M. Dent & Sons Ltd., 1983.

192

Deussen, P., *The Philosophy of the Upanishads*, New York, Dover Pub. Inc., 1966.

Dumitrescu, I. and Kenyon, J.N., *Electrographic Imaging in Medicine and Biology*, St. Helier, Jersey, Neville Spearman, 1983.

Eastcott, M.J., *'I' The Story of the Self*, London, Rider and Company, 1979.

Eastcott, M.J., *The Seven Rays of Energy*, Tunbridge Wells, Sundial House, 1980.

Elkin, A.P., *Aboriginal Men of High Degree*, St. Lucia, University of Queensland Press, 1977.

Fullerson, Mary, *The Form of the Fourth*, London, Stuart & Watkins, 1971.

Fullerson, Mary, *By a New and Living Way*, Berkeley and London, Shambhala, 1974.

Goswami, S.S., *Layayoga*, London, Routledge & Kegan Paul, 1980.

Graves, T., *Dowsing*, London, Turnstone Press, 1976.

Hall, M.P. *Man — Grand Symbol of the Mysteries*, Los Angeles, Philosophical Research Society, 1947.

Harold, P., *The Shining Stranger*, New York, Harold Institute, 1967.

Hunt, R., *The Seven Keys to Colour Healing*, Saffron Walden, C.W. Daniel Co. Ltd., 1958.

Iredell, E.C., *Colour and Cancer*, London, H.K. Lewis & Co., 1935.

Joy, B., *Joy's Way*, Los Angeles, J.P. Tarcher Inc., 1979.

Jung, C.G., *Memories, Dreams, Reflections,* London, Fontana, 1967.

Jurriaanse, A., *Bridges*, Cape South Africa, 'Sun Centre', 1978.

Karagulla, S., *Breakthrough to Creativity*, Santa Monica, De Vorss & Co., 1967.

Key, W.B., *Media Sexploitation*, New York, NAL, 1977.

Key, W.B., *The Clam-Plate Orgy*, New York, Signet, 1981.

Key, W.B., 'Subliminal Seduction', *Heart*, Spring, 1983.

Kilner, W., *The Human Aura*, New York, University Books, 1965.

Kimball, F., *The Language of ESP in Action,* Los Angeles, Private Publication.

Krieger, D., *The Therapeutic Touch*, New Jersey, Prentice-Hall, Inc., 1979.

Kunz, G., *The Curious Lore of Precious Stones*, New York, Dover Publications Inc., 1971.

Leadbeater, C.W., *Man Visible and Invisible*, Wheaton, Theosophical Publishing House, 1971.

Leonard, G., *The Silent Pulse*, New York, Bantam Books, 1978.

Long, M.F., *The Secret Science behind the Miracles*, Marina del Rey, Calif., De Vorss, 1948.

Moore, C.B., *Keely and his Discoveries*, New York, University Books, 1971.

Moskvitin, J., *Essay on the Origin of Thought*, Ohio, University Press, 1974.

Ostrander, S. and Schroeder, L., *Psychic Discoveries behind the Iron Curtain*, London, Abacus, Sphere Books, 1973.

Ouseley, S.G., *The Science of the Aura*, London, Fowler & Co., Ltd., 1949.

Ouseley, S.G., *The Power of the Rays*, London, Fowler & Co. Ltd., 1951.

Pearce, J.C., *The Crack in the Cosmic Egg*, New York, Julian Press, 1971.

Pixley, O., *The Armour of Light*, vols I & II, Cheltenham, Helios Book Service, 1971.

Regush, Nicholas M., *The Human Aura*, New York, Berkley Publishing Corp., 1974.

Von Reichenbach, K., *The Odic Force*, New York, University Books, 1968.

Richards, G., *The Chain of Life*, Rustington, L. Speight Ltd., 1954.

Saxton Burr, H. and Northrop, F., 'The electro-dynamic theory of life', *Main Currents in Modern Thought*, September 1962.

Secret of the Golden Flower, The, tr. E.C.F. Baynes, London, Routledge & Kegan Paul, 1962.

Tomlinson, H. *The Divination of Disease*, Saffron Walden, Health Science Press, 1954.

Veith, I., *The Yellow Emperor's Classic of Internal Medicine*, Berkeley and Los Angeles, University of California Press, 1966.

Vivekananda, S., *Raja Yoga*, New York, RV Centre, 1955.

Weaver, H., *Divining the Primary Sense*, London, Routledge & Kegan Paul, 1978.

Winn, M., *The Plug-In Drug*, New York, Bantam, 1977.

Woodruffe, J., *The Serpent Power*, Madras, Gonesh & Co (Madras) Private Ltd, 1958.

Young, L., *Earth's Aura*, New York, Avon, 1977.

Young, S., *Psychic Children*, New York, Pocket Books, 1977.

Index

Abbé Mermet, 142
Aborigine, 6, 10, 23, 25, 64
acupuncture, 15, 25, 84
addiction, 149
advertising, 147
allergies, 153
amaranth, 5
amethyst, 94, 182
angle rods, 133, 141
armour, 159
Armour of Light, 163
astral body, 44, 46, 153
astral double, 47
atmic, 52
Atlanteans, 40
atrophy, 27
aum, 168
aura, 1, 2, 4, 6-10, 12-20, 32, 41-4,
    47, 48, 50, 52, 65-77, 84-7, 91,
    99, 102, 103, 107, 109, 110, 115,
    117-19, 121-5, 127, 128, 130,
    133-5, 138-42, 144-6, 148, 151,
    152, 156-63, 167-9, 171-3, 178,
    182-6, 189, 190
aura layers, 67, 69, 138
aura mapping, 141
Aurameter, 133, 134
auras bonding, 155

Babbitt, Dr E., 29, 32, 33, 39, 59
Bagnall, Oscar, 74, 75, 77
Bailey, Alice, 92, 94, 107-9
Bentine, Michael, 110

Besant, Annie, 51
bindu point, 54-7
biomorphic rings, 178
biomorphs, 137, 138
black, 60, 61, 106
Blavatsky, Madame, 40, 42, 94, 108
blue, 26, 43, 47, 50, 93, 95, 100
Boehme, Jacob, 64, 92
brittle aura, 159
brown, 106
Buber, Martin, 159
buddhic, 52
Burr, Saxton, 11, 15, 88-90

Cameron, Verne, 133-5
cancer, 81, 89, 139, 150, 152
Cayce, Edgar, 44, 105, 110, 114
chakras, 27, 53, 55-64, 77, 79
chakras: base, 64; brow, 52, 60, 61,
    79; crown, 52, 61, 79; heart, 53,
    60; sacral, 53, 56, 58, 59; solar
    plexus, 53, 60; spleen, 58, 79;
    throat, 52, 56, 60
chi, 25, 37
children, 2, 3
chiropractic, 87
Chromolume, 33
chrysolite, 177
cities, 15, 17, 189
clairvoyance, 48, 65, 175
clairvoyant(s), 2, 7, 14, 31, 33, 47,
    48, 50, 58, 65, 71, 73, 75, 91,
    139

clever-men, 23
cloudbuster, 38
coccyx, 53
colour(s), 7, 24, 26, 43, 44, 91-4, 99, 102-9, 140, 121, 124, 169, 171-3, 177
colour breathing, 171
colour pass, 171
Command therapy, 81
consciousness, 1, 9, 17, 43, 45, 47, 53
copper bangle, 178
Corbin, Henry, 42, 43, 63, 129
coronal discharge, 13, 85
crystals, 9, 75, 116, 174, 175, 179, 187

Daud, 61
David, 61, 63
Davies, Paul, 56
diamond, 8, 94, 181, 187
Diane, 78-80
diaphragm, 45
dicyanin, 67, 69, 74
Don Juan, 2, 19, 113, 114
dowsing, 132, 133, 140, 142, 144
dreams, 99
drugs, 18, 152, 157
dynaspheric force, 34, 35, 37

Eastcott, Michal, 94
electricity, 11, 32
electromagnetic, 16
emanations, 31
emerald, 94, 180, 181
emotional body, 46, 94
energy, 4, 27, 36, 85
energy fields, 5, 15, 81, 83, 99, 187
etheric body, 26, 27, 45, 46, 69, 78, 86, 94

fatigue, 43
fear, 46
fire, 22, 23, 43, 53
flames, 43
flares, 91
fluoridation, 153
food additives, 153
force-field, 182

garnet, 174
gems, 175, 178-80
glass, 86, 187, 188
gold, 58, 62, 75
golden, 58, 169
gossip, 155
Graves, Tom, 132, 144
Great Invocation, 190
green, 31, 43, 60-2, 93, 94, 97, 101, 104, 156
grey, 75, 90, 106

Halo, 6, 7, 79
hand scanning, 83, 125, 143
harmlessness, 156, 188
harmony, 9, 15
Harold, Preston, 188
headgear, 8
healed, 20
healers, 9
healing, 9, 174
health, 7, 25, 74, 174
holograph, 9, 10
holographic, 10, 17
Hunt, Roland, 91, 117
hyperkinetic syndrome, 149
hypnotic, 147

immortality, 186
impressions, 145, 159, 161
indigo, 93, 99, 105
invisible, 2, 5, 9, 22, 115, 174
Iredell, Dr E.C., 169, 170
irritability, 149
irritation, 46, 186
itches, 118, 120
itch points, 122-4

jacinth, 177, 180
jade, 181, 182
jasper, 94, 182
Jesus, 7, 19, 46, 63, 164, 168, 184, 186, 188
Joy, Brugh, 81-3, 90, 125, 126
Jung, Carl, 47, 56
junk energy, 148
junk food, 34, 148, 150
Jupiter, 177

Karagulla, Shafica, 77-80, 90, 153
Keely, John, 29, 34-40
Key, Wilson Bryan, 149
Kilner, Walter, 65-7, 70-5, 77, 87, 135
Kimball, Fred, 118-24, 151, 138
kirlian, 12, 13, 84, 85, 90
Kreiger, Dolores, 172
kundalini, 56, 58, 111
kuranita, 23

lapis lazuli, 9, 178
latifa, 63
Leadbeater, C.W., 51, 58
Leo, 177
Leonard, George, 6
life-field, 6, 89, 90, 143
life-force, 10, 11, 18, 21, 23, 25, 27, 29, 31, 34, 39, 40, 45, 113, 153, 157
life-form, 4, 19
light, 1, 14, 19, 22, 26, 31, 33, 43, 63, 147, 163-9, 184-91
light, lines of, 127
lotus, 57, 62
love, 20, 161, 169
lower-self, 44, 52, 61, 184
luminosity, 32

magic, 23
magnet, 31, 116
magnetism, 11
manas, 25
mandarins, 9, 178
Mars, 177
media, 147, 149, 153
meditation, 18, 26, 47, 50
medulla oblongata, 79
mental body, 45, 48, 94
Mercury, 177
meridians, 25, 83, 84
mineral, 2, 37
mistletoe, 5
monkshood, 5
motor-force, 34
Motoyama, Dr H., 53
muscle test, 87
musk, 160
mystic, 33, 42, 63, 184

nadis, 26, 58
nervous system, 11, 26, 27, 87
Northrop, F., 11, 15, 88

od, 30, 32
odic, 30, 31
omens, 99
orange, 26, 50, 93, 97, 104, 172
orgone, 37, 38
Ouseley, S.G., 115-17
ovoid, 47, 49

parasympathetics, 59
parathyroids, 59
peace, 1
pearl, 177, 180
pendulum, 141-3
Pierrakos, John, 75-7
pineal, 45, 61, 169, 187
pituitary, 45, 60, 187
Pixley, Olive, 163-5
pollution, 16, 17, 145, 151, 189, 190
possession, 157
power, 1, 184, 191
prana, 21, 26-8, 37
pranayama, 28
prayer, 1, 47, 50
predators, 3
priests, 21
prodigal son, 57
protective circle, 162
psychic, 8, 58
psychic attack, 162
psychics, 2, 7, 66
Pulsors, 182, 183
punks, 115
purification, 19
purify, 18

radiance, 184, 185
radiated, 27
radiation(s), 27, 149
radiational couriers, 4
radiatory field, 10
Ravitz, Leonard, 89
rays, 71, 75, 91-102, 171
red, 58, 60, 61, 75, 85, 93, 95, 100, 177
Reich, Wilhelm, 29, 36, 37, 39

Reichenberg, Karl von, 29-34, 39, 65
Richards, Guyon, 136-9
Ritual of Light, 165-7
Roberts, Jane, 130
rosemary, 160
rose-pink, 106, 167
Rosicrucians, 57, 159, 160
ruby, 9, 94, 177, 178, 180, 181

sappers, 153-5
sapphire, 94, 181
Schlieren, 86-8
screen(s), 67, 69, 74, 75, 77
sensitives, 2, 31, 77, 161
sensitivity, 2, 3, 107
Seth, 130
sex, 150
shadow, 20, 186
shaman, 9, 22, 32, 41, 64, 99, 144, 175
shimmering, 76, 86
singularity, 56
solar plexus, 23, 60, 153, 167
soul, 45, 57, 94, 112, 160, 163, 184, 187
spiritual, 7, 32, 46
spleen, 46, 58
subconscious, 149
subliminal, 107, 149, 150
subtle bodies, 52, 64
Sufi, 43, 54, 92, 184, 186

tantric, 54, 56, 63
television, 148, 149
temper, 46
theosophy, 42, 51
third-eye, 64, 175, 187

thought-forms, 48, 50, 51, 145
thyroid, 80
tiki, 176
Tiller, William, 85
Tomlinson, Dr H., 132
topaz, 94
totemic, 24
transfiguration, 184
transformation, 185
transformative, 19
transforming, 19, 20
turinga, 64

unruffling aura, 173
Upanishads, 21, 26

vaccines, 138, 139
Vedas, 13
Venus, 177
vibrations, 34
violet, 75, 93, 101, 177
vitalist, 11, 29
vitality, 15, 27, 160
vitamins, 21, 28
voltmeter, 88
vortices, 78, 79

warrior, 19
Weaver, Herbert, 3, 144
white, 26, 60, 85, 177
Winn, Marie, 150

Yao, George, Dr, 182
yellow, 43, 50, 58, 60, 93, 96, 101, 104, 177
yoga, 18
yogi, 22, 54
Young, Louise, 189